Faith and the City

Faith and the City

A Memoir

A Girl's Search for
Post-College Meaning

Jennifer Ruisch

[RELEVANTBOOKS]

Published by Relevant Books
A division of Relevant Media Group, Inc.

www.relevantbooks.com
www.relevantmediagroup.com

Design by Relevant Solutions
Cover design by Ben Pieratt
Interior design by Jeremy Kennedy, Ryan Skjervem

Relevant Books is a registered trademark of Relevant Media Group, Inc., and is registered in the U.S. Patent and Trademark Office.

Scripture quotations marked (NIV) are taken from the HOLY BIBLE, NEW INTERNATIONAL VERSION®. NIV®, Copyright © 1973, 1978, 1984 by International Bible Society. Used by permission of Zondervan Publishing House. All rights reserved.

Scripture quotations marked (NLT) are taken from the Holy Bible, New Living Translation, copyright 1996. Used by permission of Tyndale House Publishers, Inc., Wheaton, Illinois 60189. All rights reserved.

Library of Congress Control Number: 2005934271
International Standard Book Number: 0-9763642-9-8

For information or bulk orders:
RELEVANT MEDIA GROUP, INC.
100 SOUTH LAKE DESTINY DR. STE. 200
ORLANDO, FL 32810
407-660-1411

06 07 08 09 10 8 7 6 5 4 3 2 1

Printed in the United States of America

For all the Marios and Juans out there. Your long hours of hard work day after day in a country that is not your home deserves far more credit. It is what inspired me to write.

Contents

Acknowledgments   ix

Introduction   xi

01   Accidental Taoists   1

02   The Possibility Prescription   15

03   The Opiate of the People   33

04   Who Is John Galt?   51

05   Trixie Sticks   65

06   Zen and the Art of Waiting Tables   77

07   A New Angle   91

08   Cook County   103

09   The Business of Belonging   117

10   The Real World   135

11   How Shall We Then Live?   159

12   The Doctor's Wisdom   173

Afterword   185

Acknowledgments

Thank you to my husband, Ryan. Your compliments mean twice as much because they are coming from someone as brilliantly intelligent and well-rounded as yourself.

Thank you to some important girls: Kerry Kennedy, your encouragement means more than you'll know. Lora Mattix, you are ridiculously smart; your advice is always dead-on. Kim Welge, you are the best sister-in-law and fellow writer/cheerleader I ever could have asked for. Dana Luke, your ability to share your heart in conversation always inspires me to grow. Kristin Kuiper, you are a talented communicator, and I've learned much from you.

My family is my best support in everything I do. Thank you Jerry and Renee Chiaramonte, Chris, Tony, Katie, Randy and Patti Ruisch, Lindsay, Marc, Kim, and Ana.

Grandma Myers and Grandma Roggen, thank you for letting me know you were praying.

Nancy Pace-Miller, you were the first person to trust me with taking words from idea to print, which was probably kind of a mistake since I plastered the faces of my friends all over the college yearbook. But you know deep down you loved it, and you also must know that you're the greatest. I'll even give a shout-out to Piston right now to prove I mean it.

Kathy Myers, without your positive encouragement I don't think I would have ever tried to write at all. Your sweet spirit and genuine smile make others believe in themselves.

And lastly, but most importantly, thank you to Erin Zimmerman, Rebekah Campanella, and Kate Kopser. Living with you girls and our myriad of experiences has obviously been the greatest source of inspiration for me. That, combined with the fact that the world is awesome enough to contain people like 21 Crow.

Introduction

> *"The link of causes and effects which now have*
> *brought us here together—they are like the sound*
> *of echoes, the sport of a game of illusion."*
> —Buddha

A homeless man I met in Dunkin' Donuts changed my life.

It was kind of like the time I bought a carton of chocolate peanut butter ice cream, and it changed my sophomore year in college.

At the onset of another school year, my roommate Sarah and I found ourselves taking our first joint trip to the grocery store closest to campus. Half the university had the same idea, giving us no choice but to execute the annoying but obligatory *"How was your summer?"* routine more times than we desired. In the frozen food aisles, Sarah kibitzed with girls from our old dorm while I loaded a carton of chocolate ice cream into our cart. Sarah suddenly stopped mid-sentence, turned to me, and said, "Could you please buy chocolate peanut butter ice cream instead of just plain chocolate?" An out-of-the-ordinary request, yet I had no reason to refuse.

In the checkout line, Sarah explained that chocolate peanut butter ice cream was Greg's favorite flavor. Greg was Sarah's recently acquired boyfriend, and she was overly eager to please him.

Because we had purchased "Greg's favorite flavor," Sarah asked if we could stop by his dorm to surprise him with an ice cream study break. I believe she actually referred to the event as a "beginning of the school year/welcome back/ice cream party," but I agreed to it despite her overzealousness.

When I entered the lobby of Greg's residence hall, I noticed a tall guy my age talking to the dorm director at the front desk. He explained he had accidentally locked himself out of his room, after which the dorm director disappeared into her office to find a master key.

He let out a long, frustrated sigh, slumped down to the carpet, pulled *Paradise Lost* out of his backpack, and opened it to a bookmarked page.

I walked toward him nonchalantly. "You locked out?"

He gave an affirmative nod without looking up. This bothered me.

"What class are you reading that for?" I asked.

"I'm not." He still refused to look up from his book.

"You seem pretty lost in it." I smirked at my pun. He did not.

"So you're reading it just for fun then?" I was relentless.

"Does it seem like I'm having fun?" He finally looked straight at me. "I got locked out of my room, and now I have to wait until somebody can let me back in. Meanwhile, some ignorant girl who thinks she's clever is trying her best to divert my attention from the profound words of a literary genius so that she and I can engage in some meaningless, semi-flirtatious banter. Does that sound like fun?"

I later learned the boy's name was Michael Vaughn. He was a social recluse who rarely left his dorm room, but that night he had accidentally locked himself out and had to go to the lobby to ask the dorm director for help.

I dated Mike the rest of my sophomore year.

Mike was a chain-smoking, Camus-reading intellect who gave impromptu lectures on anything from the origins of salt to string theory. I knew from the beginning that Mike and I wouldn't last, but his love of literature gave him a slight edge over the rest of the college boys acquiring beer bellies in tandem with business degrees. His intermittent apathy for me didn't hurt anything either. Immaturity loves a challenge.

Mike had an uncanny resemblance to Johnny Depp, in more than just appearance. His voice and mannerisms were Johnny Depp (think *Chocolat*, not *Pirates of the Caribbean*). Everyone who met Mike felt the need to tell him he reminded them of Johnny, and I felt bad for the countless well-meaning souls who fell victim to his standard reply:

> So what you're telling me is that I look like some average guy who people imagine to be larger than life just because their small minds can't separate the illusion of a big screen from reality. You're asserting that by looking like this guy, I am somehow "special" even though we're all just a pile of connected bones with skin stretched over them. We all act asinine in relationships. We're all terrified that we aren't as smart or as good-looking as the next guy. We all drool in our sleep, and we all go to the bathroom—which you have to admit is not a very glamorous thing. So, if by telling me I look like Johnny Depp, you are hoping that

I grasp some supposed inherent compliment implied in your statement—I can assure you, I don't. Your comment means absolutely nothing to me because Johnny Depp himself means absolutely nothing. In fact, all you told me by making that comment is that you yourself are very weak, belonging to the mindless mass that allows not only their viewing and reading materials, but, incredibly enough, their personal conversations, to involve silly characters—created, fictitious images made *with* a lot of money to *make* a lot of money. Had you told me that I speak like Churchill or write like Hemingway, I would have thanked you, since these men have accomplished something in life worth the breath it takes to utter their names. But instead you compared me to Johnny Depp because your culture has molded you, rather than vice versa. So although I cannot thank you for your comment, I will at least add you to the list of people I hope to never be compared to in the future. In fact, I'll put your name on my list right below Brad Pitt and right above Ben Affleck ... and the really sad thing is, you'll probably walk away from me right now feeling strangely honored instead of feeling like the miserable, bored person you are.

Although I appreciated most of Mike's diatribes, his skepticism became exhausting. I broke up with him just before summer, and we never spoke again. Nevertheless, I spent every day of my sophomore year with Mike and, thus, had hundreds of little experiences I otherwise would not have had. Like the time Mike infuriated me by not speaking to me all night—through dinner, two games of pool, and a movie. He even pointed to his entrée choice on the restaurant menu so he wouldn't have to order aloud. By the end of the night he had not uttered one solitary vowel in six hours, and I was understandably irate. As we pulled onto campus,

I yelled, "Mike, what is your problem? Do you have any idea how angry I am with you right now?" He just smiled and replied, "Was it something I said?"

If a carton of ice cream changed my sophomore year in college, I shouldn't be surprised that a homeless man in Dunkin' Donuts changed my life. Someone once said, "The fragile thread of chance upon which many relationships are spurred is astounding—but for a minute or two delay, many would have failed to meet another human being who permanently changed their entire life."

But is the Butterfly Effect really valid? Can one little choice or encounter be credited for everything that comes as a result of it? Can the time you leave the house in the morning or the route you take to work set into motion a completely different chain of events that otherwise would not have occurred? If a butterfly flapping its wings over the Atlantic can theoretically produce a typhoon in the Pacific, can't the decision to dine in rather than get takeout determine whether or not you meet your soul mate?

In the movie *Sliding Doors*, Gwyneth Paltrow's character makes one choice—to take a train home from work—that permanently changes her life. She evolves into a different person and marries a different man, simply because she caught the train. In the French film *Happenstance*, a man throws an old shoe onto the road, and the spiraling consequences of this insignificant action turn out to be of great significance. There are many more examples of this phenomenon in movies like *Serendipity*, *The Butterfly Effect*, and *Amélie*.

These movies would have me believe there's validity to the Butterfly Effect. And I honestly don't think I ever would have met Mike were it not for the ice cream. Therefore, I'm going to credit a homeless man for speaking the words I needed to hear in order to move on with my life.

Who knows—I might still be sitting in Dunkin' Donuts today had I not met him.

ONE

ACCIDENTAL TAOISTS

"There is no disaster greater than not being content."
—*Tao Te Ching*

Chicago hated me. I had felt the tension mounting between us for a while. I had entered our relationship with such high expectation for the future, and now I just felt like one of many. Overlooked. Alone. I wanted to make a T-shirt that said "The Windy City Blows."

Rachel and I moved to Chicago after college graduation, expecting to find everything there, including ourselves. Rachel hoped to find a place that felt like home with people who seemed like family, since she wasn't too keen on her own. I was just hoping to find a job that gave me greater power and status than Barney Fife. And, of course, neither of us would complain if the city were to bring us the one thing college had not: the opportunity for true love. I hadn't been in love since I was ten years old. His name was Ryan, and my journal pages from elementary school were filled with anecdotes about our young, ever-changing romance:

"Ryan stole my Trapper Keeper and my grape lip gloss today, then he

pushed me down in the snow. It was soooo awesome! Wowie Zowie!"

"Ryan asked me out today.YIPPEE! I just know in my heart that we're gonna get married someday."

It was all so pitiful—the confidence I had that I would be with Ryan, my one true love, and my use of exclamatory words ending in a long *e* sound. And what truth does a child know anyway?

When Rachel first caught a glimpse of the Chicago skyline, I remember her saying, "Now *this* is a place that holds endless possibilities." A few weeks later, I scoffed at the statement. If there were any possibilities in the city, we certainly weren't finding them. Getting out of bed every day had become a struggle in itself. Rachel and I were sleeping until noon ... sometimes later. We agreed that sleeping as long as we could was a shrewd move since the excitement of our dreams far outweighed that of our waking lives.

I had lived with Rachel throughout college. I remember coming home once at five in the morning to find four of my friends engaged in a heated game of poker at the kitchen table. I also noticed three other friends in front of the television, engrossed in a video game involving sniper rifles. Another friend was playing a rousing full-length rendition of "Free Bird" on the guitar while several others surfed the Internet to settle an argument over whether or not Demi Moore has a lazy eye. One of my old roommates was cooking stir-fry, and Rachel was busy mixing up twelve cups of her mom's gourmet hot cocoa at the dining room table.

No matter what time of day, there was always something happening in college.

Once, a group of our totally sober guy friends stopped by at midnight carrying baseball bats and wearing wife beaters under leather coats. When I opened the door, our friend Luke got within three inches of my face and shouted, "It's Caveman Day!" We had no idea what this meant at the time and to this day still don't.

"We're going to rough some people up tonight, starting with you girls!" Luke was still shouting at me in a ridiculously loud, pseudo-intimidating voice. (I say "pseudo" because everything is pseudo when you're in college.) Our friends "roughing us up" amounted to them stripping all the sheets off our beds and turning our living room furniture upside down.

College wasn't boring. If we weren't throwing a party or attending one, we were at a football game or somewhere downtown amidst the chaos of a city that boasted six universities. Not to mention boys and dating and the drama all that entailed. I remember one girl who sent dead, decaying rats via U.S. priority mail to any girl on campus she thought looked twice at her boyfriend. Unfortunately, I had several classes with him, and rumors floated around for months that I would be her next target. In the kitchen one night, I overheard Rachel say there was a lot of mail for me. Without looking up from the Ramen noodles I was stirring, I told her to set it all on the coffee table. I nearly overturned the pan of scalding water when Rachel suddenly shouted, "Rats!" I thought for sure I was going to turn my head and see several tiny rodent corpses in our living room. Instead, Rachel explained she had just received an old Psych test back in the mail and was disappointed with her score of 62 percent. Why she chose to use such an antiquated expletive I never did learn.

The girl who sent out the rat care packages was only one of many college students who entertained me (a criminal justice major) with their indiscretions that bordered on misdemeanors. Like the time some students from my Law Enforcement class visited a state penitentiary, only to learn upon arrival that five of the forty classmates in attendance could not continue the field trip because there were outstanding warrants for their arrests. [An aside: That episode served to reiterate my theory that there is a link between a student's chosen field of study and a desire to overcome personal weakness. Crazy people study psychology, sick people study medicine, guilty people study theology, and, last but not least, criminally minded people study criminal justice.]

My college classes, both criminal justice and otherwise, were intriguing, and the professors were brilliant. We hung onto their every word like self-help junkies listening to Tony Robbins. Our classroom notes may have been adorned with doodles, but somehow, the substance of the lectures always managed to seep into the crevices of our minds, irrevocably molding the way we strung our thoughts together well after it was all over.

Rachel and I met at the campus café every day between classes to debrief the day's news over mango smoothies. We'd sit on the patio and talk with (or shout at) dozens of friends and acquaintances walking around campus. There were plenty of stories about who was out with whom last weekend, who was hooking up with whom, and which football players got busted for what drugs.

We'd meet friends for dinner in the cafeteria each night, followed by a free-for-all in the library where no studying was allowed. My friend Jason and I would instead hold nightly debates over important questions such as "Who has more common sense? You or me?" or "Who has better leadership skills? You or me?" The answer was always me. But Jason was a good sport and still invited us over for his specialty chili and venison dinner despite the fact that we had hung signs all over campus advertising his phone number and the words "I'll clip your toenails for free."

The only interruption to our friendly library disputes came at nine o'clock at night when our friend Nathan would get down on the library carpet on all fours and bleat like a goat—loudly—for approximately thirty seconds. This was done to temporarily stop any studying that might actually be taking place in the library. It was also done for the ensuing comedy, as dozens of library assistants made a clean sweep of the building, trying to locate "the goat" once and for all. Luke insisted that Nathan was a Lebanese spy masquerading as a harmless, funny college student. "He's going to divert your attention one night with his little goat show, but meanwhile he'll have a bomb planted somewhere in the library ready to detonate." There was no shortage of entertainment, no matter how juvenile.

After saying goodbye to friends at college graduation, Rachel and I had a not-so-bright idea. We had no post-college plans, and a move to a big city sounded good, but I loathed L.A. and Rachel hated New York.

"What about Chicago?" I asked.

Rachel shrugged. "Sounds good. Let's move there."

I think that was the extent of our rationale and the end of our discussion. Sure, we had no jobs or place to live, but those were minor details.

For some reason, the only clear memory I have of that dreaded day is that we rolled into Chicago blasting a Counting Crows CD. I should have guessed that such a melancholy prelude wouldn't pave the way to unending post-college bliss. But our spirits were high, and why shouldn't they have been? Within two hours we had leased a space in a beautiful brownstone built in 1882 in the Lincoln Park neighborhood, the "place to be" for twentysomethings in Chicago.

Our first few weeks in the city were a barrage of new sensory input. We played tourist, visiting museums and blues clubs, learning the L routes and the differences between neighborhoods, and brushing shoulders with local celebrities like Ronnie "Woo Woo" Wickers (the unofficial mascot of the Chicago Cubs since the 1960s).

We attended hip-hop open-mic nights and listened to local rappers extol the virtues of good old Chi-town. One night an emcee called "The Next Thing" rapped for ten minutes about how Chicago was going to be the starting point for world peace and how The Next Thing himself would be leading the movement to teach all men to embrace each other as brothers. A half hour after his performance, The Next Thing threw a punch at a rival emcee and was quickly escorted from the building.

Chicago might not have been the starting point for world peace, but we still thought it was a rather magical place. Rachel and I loved attending citywide movie nights every week in Grant Park. We watched old Gene Kelly classics with the warm breeze and skyscrapers surrounding us. We went to the Green Mill, the home of the original poetry slam, and listened to poetry that left us in tears. We frequented Kingston Mines, since it was just a few blocks from our apartment, and we found it produced the best blues and hot wings ever. We often sat in the actual park for which Lincoln Park was named—an expanse of green along the lakefront that continually smelled like freshly cut grass and wildflowers. We gazed at the stretch of beach that separated Lake Michigan and its sailboats from the postcard-perfect Chicago skyline. Then we walked the block back to our apartment, knowing that, given our surroundings, we should be deliriously happy. But then we'd see groups of laughing friends, and we'd remember we were alone.

Rush Street was the worst. Massive crowds of strangers on a Friday night were a poor substitute for the old college social gatherings with hundreds of recognizable faces. Walking past the restaurants where people lounged on outdoor patios, telling stories over fruity drinks, made us wonder where we had gone wrong. How had everyone else in the city found a circle of friends when a social life was eluding us altogether?

The only human interaction we had each night was with the Huxtibles, Keatons, Bunkers, and Barones. We also had become well-acquainted with the residents of a certain California zip code—90210. We spent hours discussing Dylan's nuances, Donna and

David's rocky relationship, Kelly's uncharacteristic coke addiction, and Brandon's latest student government debacle. (Didn't it seem like there was always a political theme when it came to Brandon?) My old boyfriend Mike would have detested the new me. It felt like Adam Duritz's lyrics were finally proving true: "I don't need anyone these days, I feel like I'm fading away."

Before Rachel and I moved to Chicago, we had sent out a combined total of fifty-one resumés to prospective employers. We never received even one call. My mom suggested we both take minimum-wage jobs—for survival's sake.

"Mom." I tried to stay calm. "I have a *degree* ..." My voice was getting uncontrollably louder. "I am not going to work a job that some dumb high-school kid could do *when I have a degree in criminal justice.*" The whole idea of working for minimum wage after spending four years and $75,000 on an education felt more shameful than wearing a fur coat to a PETA convention. Plus, Rachel had interned at a celebrated mental health facility while earning her psychology degree, and I had worked all through college as a counselor for juvenile delinquents. We had degrees *and* experience; we weren't going to take a job beneath us. I was indignant: "It would be a waste of my life to take some dumb retail job, Mom—you know it would. And *please* don't even suggest that I start waiting tables."

Without college cafeteria food at our disposal, we soon learned we lacked culinary skills. Rachel's dinner routine consisted of peanut butter eaten from the jar with a fork (our three spoons were perpetually dirty). Dessert was chocolate frosting from a tube. I, on the other hand, made my requisite Ramen noodles and washed them down with a cup of hot chocolate. Our days consisted of a lackluster diet and ample sleep in our dark apartment. Our daily dialogue sounded like a B movie starring two stoners. "No way! That is the *third* time today I've heard someone on TV reference Laurence Fishburne. That is so random! Can you believe how synchronistic that is?" We also spent a lot of time playing "the Catholic Channel game"—our own invention. We took turns muting Mother Angelica and making up pretend sermons to correspond with her different facial expressions. If she looked angry, we might preach hellfire and brimstone; if she looked peaceful, we might preach on the saints.

With no day jobs or nightlife, our biggest excitement was playing hide and seek with a peeping Tom outside our apartment window. The nights he'd show up, we could see his shadow on the alley wall. At first we were a little shaken up. Then we became angry and ready to take action. So I, like the ignorant criminal justice graduate I was, ran outside to try to catch him. I'm not sure what I planned to do once I caught him, but fortunately for me, he always managed to get away. Finally, we took a proactive and creative approach to the situation: we left a note for the peeping Tom penned in colored markers that said, "Welcome, make yourself at home in the alley." Next to the note we left a plate of cookies. The guy never returned.

When there was nothing to watch on television, we watched *Reality Bites* on VHS in an attempt to make our post-college, directionless lives seem fairly normal, if not slightly en vogue. "All you have to be by the age of twenty-three is yourself," Ethan Hawke's character said. His words brought us a small degree of comfort. We were twenty-two, and if our only duty in the next year was to "become ourselves," we may have found a viable goal.

I asked Rachel why the age twenty-three was so significant. "Dave Matthews sings, 'Twenty-three and so tired of life'; Coolio sings, 'I'm twenty-three now, but will I live to see twenty-four?' So what's the big deal with twenty-three?"

Rachel answered (after first chastising me for citing Coolio as a viable reference), "Maybe twenty-three is the age people become disillusioned with life. Until twenty-three, everything is preparation for a 'life' that's supposed to begin after college. But when you finally get to twenty-three, you realize there really isn't life after college."

Why else would John Mayer need to scream at the top of his lungs, "I just found out there's no such thing as a real world"?

But unlike John, we couldn't rise above the lie, and the city continued to swallow us whole. John also sang, "It might be a quarter-life crisis." And indeed it was. It seemed like life had been a continual climb to reach a phantom peak that was actually just a plateau. Were we supposed to keep climbing and expending more energy? What for?

The enormity of figuring out what to do with ourselves had paralyzed us. We felt like we had given the responsible and meaningful adult life a good old (post-) college try. But we had failed. Thus, we became accidental Taoists. We did less and less each day, until finally we arrived at complete and total non-action. I had read *Tao Te Ching* in college and been interested in its postulations. It suggested that by doing nothing, a person actually accomplishes everything. I now had time to test this wisdom.

Rachel suggested we take drastic measures to solve our problems. Like move. She said that moving back home to live with her parents in Minnesota didn't sound so bad.

I told her people rarely *solve* their problems—they usually just *outgrow* them. Rachel accused me of quoting something I had read and trying to pass it off as my own thought. I pleaded guilty as usual but assured her it didn't change the fact that if we continued to wait, we would outgrow this stage, and something good would happen. Patience was the best remedy for trouble, right?

But after waiting one month, our spirits and bank accounts were empty. Ramen noodles and peanut butter were cheap dinners, but our rent was $1,300 a month. We discussed various ways to obtain rent money, from the obvious—asking our parents for help—to the creative—asking a neighborhood drug dealer for a loan (we liked innovation).

"He isn't just any drug dealer," I clarified to Rachel. "His name is Goldie, and he assured me he has very 'high-level street cred in Chi-town.'"

Goldie had whistled at me as I passed him one day on the sidewalk. At the time, he was wearing a gold shirt, gold pants, gold shoes, and a gold turban—an ensemble that complemented his mouthful of gold teeth. I refused to make eye contact with him, but he approached me nonetheless.

"Girl, you're fine," he informed me with squinted eyes and a brow furrowed as though it made him angry. "How about you and me have a nice romantic dinner tonight?"

I wasn't sure why he had posed such a rhetorical question and answered with a roll of my eyes.

"Tell you what," he said, "I'll give you this if you go to dinner with me ... just once is all I'm asking."

"This" happened to be a wad of hundred dollar bills he had extracted from his left pocket.

"I'm holding $3,000 in my hand, baby," Goldie said. "It's all yours if you'll let me take you out."

I laughed and walked away, while he shouted, "I'm telling you, baby girl ... you'll regret this!"

Wondering why the wicked prosper, I said to Rachel, "If we need to track him down, I'm sure it wouldn't be that hard to locate Chicago's one-and-only Goldie."

"How about we just ask Dan for a rent extension?" Rachel suggested. Dan was our gregarious and laudably generous landlord.

We agreed this was the best option.

After more than a month of unemployment, Rachel and I thought we caught lucky breaks when, in the same week, we were approached separately with some interesting "job opportunities." A twentysomething stranger named Edd Grosse had handed Rachel his business card. I thought it pretty gross that Edd's first name had two *d*'s (I called it a warning sign, but Rachel called me paranoid). Edd asked Rachel if she would be interested in learning some state-of-the-art self-defense techniques and then helping him teach the techniques to kids in Chicago high schools. He promised her a sizable salary and benefits, so she agreed to meet him at a neighborhood Thai restaurant later that day to "strategize and talk job specifics."

When Rachel arrived, Edd thanked her for coming and then said, "Look, I'll just be honest ..." He stared at her intently. "I'm attracted to your attractiveness," he said. Yes, *that* was his big come-on line. Not "I'm attracted to your eyes ... your smile ... your personality ..." Even "your body" would have been more forgivable. But no, he was attracted to her attractiveness. Doubtless he had a PhD in romancing women. Rachel let him pay for lunch and then gave him a fake phone number.

Since I had made fun of Rachel's encounter with Edd, it served me right when a few days later I met a man named Danny Daniels at the bank. He wanted to hire me to be his "personal assistant," promising me $20 an hour if I would take notes at his real-estate luncheons. I attended my first lunch meeting with Danny and three local developers. The first clue that I wasn't simply there to take notes came when Danny introduced me to the developers as "his friend" rather than his assistant. And it became crystal clear within minutes that Danny wanted the men to think I was more than a friend.

My weakness was not that I was a trusting, naïve person by nature. It was that I embraced anything weird and out of the ordinary. On top of that, people simply weren't scary to me. Even scary people weren't scary to me. I therefore had a tendency to get into some bad situations. Maybe I loved the challenge of getting out of them, or maybe I felt that invincibility so characteristic of youth. But whatever it was, these tendencies had led me to become a paid escort for one day. From that point on, I told Rachel that we would not befriend anyone with a weird name.

What stung the most was that we had finally experienced a few days of hope, only to have it dashed by the realization that the city was full of idiots. We were back to our dismal, meaningless existence—no job, no money, no friends, no hope.

Just when I thought things couldn't get much worse, they did. The first time I did laundry in our new building, I threw four enormous piles of clothing—including all forty pairs of underwear I owned—into the washers. (Yes, I'm one of those "wait until you run out of underwear to do the laundry" people.) I returned an hour later to switch the loads to the dryers, only to find that all my clothes had been stolen—even my forty pairs of underwear.

I was most distraught, however, over the loss of my favorite pair of jeans. I was near tears when I broke the news to Rachel. I had worn the same rust-colored shirt and bell-bottomed jeans literally every single day since we moved to Chicago. It was a kind of silent protest to the fact that there was nothing and no one to get dressed up for.

"You mean the jeans you wear every single day got stolen too?" Rachel's eyes were apologetic. "The jeans you originally bought for Surf Day?"

A few of our college friends were big-time surfers and had deemed one day a year "Surf Day," during which we all wore mandatory "surf attire" (a definition open to interpretation). In retrospect, the theme days we adhered to in college were definitely absurd, but I was still distressed that my foremost token of that absurdity had been taken from me without warning.

I was never the type of girl to worry about clothes, so aside from my Surf Day jeans, my losses weren't worth a belabored grieving period. Most of my clothes had been vintage—literally from the Salvation Army, DAV, or Goodwill. Nevertheless, I had to buy all new underwear—an unforeseen cost that further depleted my financial resources. It wasn't the clothes I was most angry about; it was that I hadn't caught the thief in the act. After four years of studying crime, I assumed I would have at least been vigilant enough to stop it.

A week later, I got into a verbal sparring match with a group of frat boys stumbling home from a bar on our street. They were mad that I had taken a parking space they said was "reserved for Tim." I later realized that the guys had planned to stand in an available parking space (in all their drunken glory) until Tim could navigate his jeep there, past the cabs that lined our street. At least, that had been their plan until I pulled up and cut Tim off. Open parking spaces in Lincoln Park and other north-side neighborhoods were rare, and finding one could be as thrilling as waking up from a nap on a plane to find the beverage cart at your aisle. So I naturally pulled into the open parking spot, only to meet with a slew of curse words and threats of bodily harm.

"You stole Tim's space! That's Tim's space!" One particularly large blond jock stumbled around, shouting at me and waving both middle fingers.

"It's my space now," I said. "Tell Tim that if he wants space he can go to the moon." With those parting words, I walked into my apartment. After I went inside, Tim's friends knocked off my car's side view mirrors, shattered my windshield, and stole my collection of 150 CDs.

Oops.

Note to self: Do not attempt to put overly cocky frat boys in their place, especially when they are wasted and looking to kick some …

Assuming a person could easily go to Best Buy and replace all the stolen CDs, my loss shouldn't really have been a huge ordeal. However, my particular CD collection could not be repurchased. It was priceless, much like my Surf Day jeans. My CDs were a burned musical diary of my entire life from junior high to the present—from Mr. Big to Norah Jones. Nowhere else could I find Miles Davis, Def Leopard, and 10,000 Maniacs sharing the same vinyl. As days passed, I grew more depressed over the loss of my life's soundtrack. My past had been erased, and my present was a poor substitute.

"Let's move." It was the only suggestion Rachel ever seemed to offer.

"Move where?" I asked.

"Back to …" I didn't let her finish her sentence.

"Don't even say it, Rachel," I said. "I refuse to be that alumni—still hanging out on campus all the time. We would look like such losers."

"We are such losers," she said.

Rachel always knew how to make me feel better.

TWO

THE
POSSIBILITY
PRESCRIPTION

"The sage wears clothes of coarse cloth but carries jewels in his bosom."
—*Tao Te Ching*

The only acquaintance we had made since moving to Chicago was a guy named Damien, whom we only met when he relieved himself at one in the morning on the bushes in front of our apartment. We thought his action was grounds for interrogation, and learned that he was originally from England and was presently headed to a party down the street. He told us the party would be very diverse (i.e., not full of drunken white frat boys), so we agreed to go with him and check it out. He was right—the party was like a UN summit with every possible country represented. In other words, the party was full of drunken internationals. Our personal negotiations were limited to India (represented by good-natured joke-teller Shiva) and France (embodied by demonstrative narcissist Fredricko). These two cornered us the moment we walked in and followed us each time we tried to mingle freely. Eventually we asked to be left alone, but they wouldn't surrender. Then we tried hiding from them on the roof deck, but they flanked us from the left stairwell. After about an hour of the French and Indian War, we decided it was time to put an end to our international networking à la Damien. On our way out the door, we stopped to say goodbye to Damien, who was conversing with a girl from the UK. She apparently didn't believe the story Damien had just finished telling her. "Damien," we overheard her say, "I can't believe it ... are you taking a piss?"

Our night ended the same way it began.

Obviously lacking for friendships, Rachel and I invited several college friends to come stay with us in Chicago. Their visit was only a temporary alleviation, but it was worth it. One of our best laughs came at a high price. While we were downtown one night, a man stopped our visiting friend Luke to ask if he would like a shoeshine. Luke said no, but the man was insistent and followed him down the street, singing, "Come on and let me make your shoes shine ... all it will take is two minutes of your time." Luke, not being very city-savvy, gave in and threw his left shoe up on a bench. The shoeshine took only two minutes, as promised. While the man worked, he sang about Luke's soon-to-be "shiny black Pimpitrons," which were going to "gleam like the sides of the Hancock building" (which we coincidentally happened to be standing under). When the man finished, he said, "That will be $25 a shoe, and the tip is up to you." We expected Luke to smile, throw him a $5 bill, and walk away, but Luke actually paid the swindler $50 in full. When the man said, "And how about a tip to keep me rollin'?" Luke then handed him $5.

We teased Luke the rest of the week: "Hey, your Pimpitrons look like they just had a $55 shoe shine." Luke told us he would "declare our friendship officially over" unless we took him to dinner at a nice restaurant to make up for the incident. We weren't sure why we were being punished for the creativity of a total stranger, but we bought him dinner anyway, so that he wouldn't harbor bitterness against our city or us. We told him he could leave the tip, though. "You want to keep our waiter rollin'—right, Luke?" I asked.

After our friends left, Rachel and I found ourselves with ample free time yet again (i.e., all day, every day). Remembering how lonely our lives had been, we decided to become regulars at a neighborhood establishment just to be around people. It was also the perfect chance to soak up some sunlight since our first-story apartment welcomed about as much sun as a medieval dungeon. We started paying daily afternoon visits to the Dunkin' Donuts next to our apartment.

We chose Dunkin' Donuts mostly because it was a stone's throw from our place, but also because the donut shop itself possessed two inherently good qualities. First, there was a Baskin-Robbins attached to it. Rachel and I had been addicted to Baskin-Robbins' Mocha Blasts throughout college, and we were ready to fall off the wagon and take up drinking them again. Upon relapsing, I mused to Rachel, "We may not be having a blast in Chicago, but at least we're having a Blast in Chicago."

The second reason we chose Dunkin' Donuts (even over first-rate options such as Starbucks, Caribou Coffee, and Einstein Bros. Bagels) was the "Trixie factor." Lincoln Park Trixies did not frequent Dunkin' Donuts.

Trixies and their male counterparts, known as Chads, were the primary dwellers of the Lincoln Park neighborhood. Trixies were sorority girls who moved to Chicago en masse, post-graduation. From Alpha to Zeta they arrived in the city to do one of two things: begin work at their first real job (and I do mean first), or ride the wave of daddy's never-ending cash flow all the way into graduate school and beyond. They owned more Kate Spade purses than Kate Spade herself; they swarmed Bally's every night in matching workout ensembles; and, above all, they were extreme *Sex and the City* fanatics. They loved Miranda's sarcastic wit, Charlotte's good conscience, and Samantha's lack thereof, but they idolized everything Carrie Bradshaw. This meant they liked to order Cosmos, spend $500 on Manolo Blahniks, and indulge in a little smoking vice. The only time Trixies ventured out of Lincoln Park was to shop the Magnificent Mile or "go to a Cubs game"—really code for "go barhopping in Wrigleyville *after* the game in hopes of meeting countless identical frat boys to hook up with."

I once overheard a Trixie describing the Lincoln Park culture to an out-of-town visitor:

> No seriously, Lincoln Park is, like, the best neighborhood in Chicago. It's just an extension of college because, like, all the sorority sisters and frat brothers still live together. But the thing is ... it's *sooo* much better than college because it's *all* the college graduates from Big Ten schools in Wisconsin, Ohio, Indiana, Iowa, Michigan, and Illinois. Getting a date is, like, so (expletive) easy because there are tons of guys, and they, like, all actually have money now. So hot frat boys will buy you sushi and cosmos every night of the week, so you can save your own money to spend at Louis Vuitton ... which, did I mention, is within walking distance? Omigawd, *everything* is within walking distance to Lincoln Park—the loop, Navy Pier, Wrigley Field, and, most importantly, the North Avenue beach house—where all the hotties hang out. It's, like, spring break all year round! But the best part is that if you live in Lincoln Park, you can, like, stumble home from tons of great bars with awesome drink specials every night of the week. People say the motto for Lincoln Park is "boys, bars, and beyond," and it's, like, *so* totally true.

The only detail she failed to mention was that most Trixies take entry-level jobs in marketing, but that was probably self-evident by her spiel. (The infamous marketing agency Leo Burnett was rumored to be crawling with more Trixies than a Lincoln Park bar on dollar-draft night.)

Then there were the Chads. These were formulaic former frat fools. You might find them calling out obscure shot names to bartenders while rehashing college war stories with their bros in Irish pubs on any given Monday.

Upon their arrival to Lincoln Park, Chads began immediately building their portfolios by working inhumane hours in hopes of skipping a rung on the corporate ladder. They reeked of Dolce & Gabbana cologne and believed that tapas and sangria sounded like an original and clever date idea. And every last one of them, regardless of appearance or capacity for animalistic behavior, still managed to land countless dates—because the Trixies were so plentiful (and so willing).

All that to say, Dunkin' Donuts was not trendy enough, expensive enough, nor elitist enough for the Trixie civilization to infiltrate. Which made it the perfect place for Rachel and me to spend our days.

We sat at our favorite sidewalk table at Dunkin' Donuts. Sometimes we read books like *In Praise of Idleness*, by Bertrand Russell, to lessen our sense of futility. I read aloud, "We have adopted the mistaken belief that work is a virtue. While work is essential for survival, it does not contribute as much to our well-being as we may think." I agreed enthusiastically with Bertrand—although by reading books such as *In Praise of Idleness*, I recognized that I was paradoxically adhering to the advice of Thomas a Kempis: "Never be entirely idle. But either be reading or writing or praying or meditating or endeavoring something for the public good." I wasn't ready to pray or meditate yet, but at least I could read rather than watch *90210*.

"Do you remember when Chris got kicked out of a Dunkin' Donuts in Boston for yelling at an employee?" Rachel asked. Reminiscing about college was one of the few activities that made us momentarily happy.

"He was so mad because they were out of something he wanted, right?" I asked. I actually remembered the story in full, but it was more fun to drag the memory out, piece by piece. It killed time and kept me in a pleasant, pre-Chicago state of mind.

"They were out of glazed donuts ... *and* coffee. Totally out," Rachel recalled.

"And wasn't it 7:00 a.m.? How could they possibly eighty-six the two Dunkin' Donuts staples at 7:00 a.m.?" I asked. "Weren't we driving back from New York City?"

I could hear Chris' gruff, angry voice in my mind, so I mimicked it for Rachel. "Dunkin' Donuts should not be this complicated!" My impersonation was dead-on and made Rachel laugh before defending him: "We have to cut him a break. He was so crazy that day because he ran out of cigarettes while we were standing in Times Square waiting for the ball to drop. Remember? He was picking up cigarette butts off the street, trying to smoke them ..."

I gagged at the thought.

Ahhh, college ... when life's biggest frustrations didn't involve the pressures of finding a job and a life, but rather of finding caffeine and nicotine.

After a few weeks of frequenting Dunkin' Donuts, Rachel and I gained the status of "daily regulars." With this standing came perks like modest discounts and a staff that knew us by name and kept our favorite table open for our 2:00 p.m. arrival.

We developed a mutual respect for the other Dunkin' Donuts regulars as well. One regular was Laura, an obsessive-compulsive who wrote on hundreds of recipe cards, then sorted and stacked them every afternoon for hours. We would wave and smile at her, but we never did learn what was written on those cards. On the saner side of things, Ian and Paul were two garbage men who made a daily stop at Dunkin' Donuts for coffee and small talk. Waste management was an interesting business, and we liked hearing stories about their routes, especially since our apartment was one of their stops. There were also a couple dozen taxi drivers who were faithful customers and had deemed the twenty-four-hour restaurant an informal headquarters of sorts. They gathered there to trade information and stories in between carting passengers around. Rachel and I spent a lot of time eavesdropping on their tales.

"Another driver was murdered last night, Rick. That makes 112 cabbies killed in Chicago in the last decade," a cab driver said. "We're pretty sure these recent murders were the work of Latino gangs." We had no idea that driving a cab was such a dangerous job. By listening in, we learned how to lease a cab car without getting ripped off, which days and times were best for driving, and which neighborhoods promised to deliver the most money. We finally understood why the streets of Lincoln Park were a mirage of marigold, seven nights a week. Driving a cab could be lucrative if you had the patience to tote a bunch of spoiled rich kids between bars (heaven knows they wouldn't dream of taking the bus). Our favorite taxi driver, Umer from Pakistan, detailed his horror stories of Lincoln Park kids getting sick, getting out of the car without paying, and getting it on in the back seat of his cab.

There were also a few daily regulars who literally called Dunkin' Donuts home. The staff was kind to these homeless patrons, who were able to come and go throughout the day to escape the cold or heat. The most visible of the bunch was the self-proclaimed "Black Jesus." He told us he used to be married, with a high-paying job, but now he was "divorced with a homeless issue." He believed each race has its own Jesus that they must follow. However, when we asked how many total Jesuses there were, he said there were only two—White Jesus and himself. He also believed that the sign of the apocalypse would be "something flying over North America in the middle of November." We pressed him for details as to what that "something" might be, but he would only say, "It's not a bird, and it's not an eagle." He repeated that sentence at least five times before we finally accepted that the sign of the apocalypse, for the time being, would have to remain a mystery.

Black Jesus had a good friend named Ben, who was about seventy, ghastly thin, and pale. He refused to button up his plaid shirt, no matter how cold it got outside. He had a trash bag full of belongings that he asked us to watch for him whenever he left the restaurant.

Our first prolonged interaction with Ben was amusing, to say the least. He helped himself to an empty chair at our table and said, "I've been meaning to ask you two young ladies ... do you rap?"

Rachel and I burst into uncontrollable laughter.

After regaining my composure, I decided to play along. "I freestyle-rap pretty well. Why do you ask?"

"Well, you see, I actually own a hip-hop record label, and I write lyrics for a lot of the recording artists you young ladies might know. Ever heard of Tupac? What about Snoop? I write all the lyrics for their songs."

By this time Rachel had also regained composure. "Which label do you own?" she asked.

"It's called Ben Records, part of Death Row. You wanna hear some sample lyrics?"

My only thought was, is this man really going to rap aloud right here, right now?

The answer to my question, I soon learned, was: absolutely.

"Dis is da way I be frontin' yo' flow—dis is my ice and yo' check my dough ..." Ben was literally shouting these lyrics at us, while trying to keep a steady beat.

Oh, and did I fail to mention that Ben was a seventy-year-old *white* man?

Rachel squeezed my knee under the table to keep me from guffawing. The whole scene was a bit surreal, and every patron stared at us with a look that said, "Shut your psycho friend up, will ya?" But Ben continued on with more rhymes about "thuggin' like dis" while "creepin' like dat" and "rollin' on dubs" while "smokin' big killa." He had thug-like hand motions to accompany every phrase he belted out, and he even threw up a couple legitimate gang signs to boot. After his big lyrical finish about "poppin' Crys in his Escalade," I began to wonder if maybe he *had* written every rap song known to man—after all, he had covered all the basics from hos to Hennessy.

"Actually, I'm not only into hip-hop," Ben said. "I'm also a well-known cartoonist. Have you young ladies ever heard of Charlie Brown?" We assured him we had. "I created Charlie Brown. Even now I can draw groovy cartoons in just seconds and then sell them to people for big money. Wanna see?" Again his question was merely perfunctory. Without hesitation, Ben took a napkin from our table and drew a stick figure on it, followed by a little copyright symbol in the bottom left-hand corner. "I drew this C sign here just like they do in books. It's so you ladies won't try to sell this napkin as your own work. The C stands for 'can't sell as your own work.' You ladies have a nice day now." And like that, he was gone.

After Ben left, I turned to Rachel and let out a long sigh of relief. "Thank God Ben copyrighted that picture. You can't draw something that *groovy* and not take the proper precautions." Rachel let out a feeble laugh, apparently still recovering from the novelty that was Ben.

The truly funny part was that we later actually befriended Ben (after first strictly prohibiting a sequel to his public rap performance). Ben was funny and harmless, and we treated him to a Dunkaccino every now and then. He, in turn, introduced us to some of his other homeless friends. We met Robert, a man who recently had been laid off at work and lost his apartment, wife, and kids shortly thereafter. He was searching for a new job to provide steady income for rent. We met Crazy Grace, who sometimes wore what looked to be a Little Red Riding Hood costume—including a long, hooded red cape. Grace continually mumbled under her breath—a lot of her incoherent ramblings sounded like lines from Shakespeare—and, living up to her name, was actually too crazy to engage in conversation. We met Scarface, a saxophone player who spent his nights making music for bar hoppers along Lincoln Avenue. He was trying to support two sons through his music and his job selling *StreetWise*, the Chicago newspaper produced and sold by the local homeless population. It was nice to run into all our new friends out and about in the neighborhood.

Then one Thursday afternoon, Ben introduced us to Dr. Porter.

Dr. Porter was an unshaven man in his sixties with shoulder-length black hair that was just showing the first signs of gray. Even though it was a warm, sunny day, he wore a long black trench coat with the collar turned up and belt tied tight. With his dark, oversized sunglasses and black beret pulled low over his forehead, he was clearly attempting to redefine the word "shady." Standing next to Ben with his loose, unbuttoned shirt, the two made quite the contrasting pair.

"This is my good friend, Dr. Porter," Ben announced proudly, with a slight Vanna White hand motion. "He owns his own business."

Dr. Porter stood, brooding silently over our table.

"Nice to meet you," I said. I offered a hand, but he didn't shake it.

After a long three-second pause, Dr. Porter finally spoke. "I've decided I'm going to give you two girls a map to my store." He handed Rachel a hand-drawn map on a piece of loose-leaf notebook paper.

On the center of the map was a red star with the words "Possibility Place" and an address.

"What kind of store is this—a bookstore?" I asked.

Dr. Porter spoke with a voice much too sweet for his abrasive appearance. "No, it's not a bookstore, but a lot of learning happens there. As you can see, it's called the Possibility Place. It's a place where you come to learn all the possibilities life has to offer."

"What if you don't think life has any possibilities to offer?" I asked. Rachel kicked me under the table; it was a distinct "let's not provoke the freaky guy in black" kick.

Dr. Porter replied graciously, "My question would be, which possibilities have you been searching for? Sometimes it's not the tangible, visible things you need in this life." He spoke slower. "Sometimes the possibilities our lives hold are for much richer, better things ... like expansion of knowledge, wisdom, understanding, perspective, relationship."

I was impressed by his miniature motivational speech, regardless of how ethereal it was.

"So this business of yours ... it's a consulting company?" I asked. "You're a life coach, right?"

I noticed that sometimes people who wanted to offer a service for money but didn't have one to offer embraced the title "life coach," charging $100 an hour to help people reach their goals. As much as I had mocked it, perhaps it was what I needed.

"No, no, I'm not a life coach," Dr. Porter said, smiling. "But if you stop by the Possibility Place this afternoon, I'll show you what I do."

"We'll try our best to make it," Rachel said.

"It's Thursday afternoon. Shouldn't you ladies be at work?" Dr.

Porter asked.

"They don't have jobs ..." Ben cut in, trying to impress his friend with insider information.

Rachel explained, "We're looking for something in our fields. We just graduated from college."

"And what are you doing in the meantime?" Dr. Porter asked.

"We sit here and drink Mocha Blasts all day." I toasted the air with my cup.

"That's no good," Dr. Porter frowned. "What if you never get a job in your field?"

"Wait ..." Rachel said, "I thought you were all about possibilities? What's up with the sudden negativity?"

I agreed. "That's some pretty poor marketing for your store, Porter." I hadn't meant to rhyme.

Dr. Porter responded, "I'm not being negative; I'm just being realistic. What if you never find jobs in your field?"

"We're not settling for anything less," Rachel said.

Dr. Porter chuckled to himself. "Ahh ... but what if something *less* is actually *more*?"

"I'm not good with riddles," I said. "Just tell us what you're trying to say."

Dr. Porter's voice grew louder and more urgent: "You girls need to do something, anything. Possibilities only come to those who don't sit around feeling sorry for themselves. You must do something today."

He pulled his trench coat tighter, something I hadn't thought possible. "Come by this afternoon when you're done here."

The way he said "done here" sounded a bit condescending, as though he didn't think our daily Dunkin' Donuts ritual was entirely essential.

Then Dr. Porter left, and we never saw him again.

One day I asked Ben why he never brought Dr. Porter around anymore, and Ben said, "Doctor who?"

Rachel and I looked at Dr. Porter's map and saw that his "store" was on a street just four blocks north of our apartment. I asked Rachel if we could go check it out. She thought I was joking. I told her we had never ventured very far north of our apartment, so it would be more of a sightseeing opportunity than anything else. "Rachel, you know deep down you're dying to visit his store," I teased. "Wasn't it you who said this city holds 'endless possibilities'? Oooh ... maybe *Dr. Porter* is your soul mate ... and you guys are destined to run the Possibility Place together. Rachel, you can't let your soul mate slip through your fingers just like that." She agreed to a quick walk just to shut me up.

We easily found the address on the map. It was a large store with gigantic glass windowpanes. There was no sign out front, and, judging by the size of the cobwebs inside, the place had been abandoned for months, maybe even years. Inside, trash was piled high on the floor. Every business in Lincoln Park was usually kept in immaculate condition, so we were surprised the city hadn't done anything about such an eyesore.

"Well, this confirms two things," I said to Rachel. "Dr. Porter is *not* a doctor ... but he definitely needs one." We turned to leave.

On the way home, Rachel performed a parody of Dr. Porter's rousing "do something, anything" speech. "Okay, I get it," I said. "The guy's a loony. But you do have to admit there might be a little sense in what he was saying." I recognized a smart suggestion when I heard one, even if it did sound extremely simplistic and unsophisticated.

"No," Rachel said. "I don't have to admit that a homeless man claiming to have a PhD makes any sense."

"All I'm saying is that maybe we should just do something, even if it isn't what we've been waiting for. Maybe doing something small could set the wheels in motion for us, you know?" Rachel said she didn't know. I suggested that in the four-block walk from the Possibility Place back to our apartment, we go into every retail store and restaurant we passed—and ask for job applications. "Baby steps," I said.

Rachel didn't want to participate at first, but after she overheard the manager at the Gap talk about the employee discount, she reneged. In a span of four blocks, we picked up applications from the Gap, American Eagle, Paronelli's Pasta, Mama's Tacos, Smoothie City, and other places that typically employed a high percentage of high-school kids.

Within two days, Rachel got hired at the Gap, and I got a job at Paronelli's Pasta, a popular hole-in-the-wall neighborhood restaurant. I called my mom to let her know that I had divorced my superiority complex and would indeed be waiting tables.

The same day I got the call about Paronelli's, I received another interesting phone call. "Hi, you don't know me, but my name is Dave, and I live in Des Plaines. I wondered ... did you happen to lose some CDs?" I was confused. "I had a bunch of CDs stolen from my car a while back ... why?"

"Well, I have them, and I'm coming to the city tonight if you want me to drop them off."

This had to be a joke—or could my thief have had a conversion experience?

"Why do you have my CDs?" I was still too skeptical to get excited.

"Well, it's kind of a long story ... but I was out jogging the other day, and I saw a CD case under some bushes in my neighbor's yard. They told me it wasn't theirs, so I looked through it to try to find the owner. One of the CDs had a label on it that said, 'Memories of our Junior Year, from Grant Tristan.' So I looked up every Grant

Tristan in the White Pages online and called them one by one. I asked every Grant, 'Did you ever burn a CD for someone and title it "Memories of our Junior Year"?'"

This guy was serious.

"After six strikes, I finally found the right Grant. He gave me your name. I repeated the process ... and that's my story."

I was dumbfounded. I hadn't talked to Grant Tristan since junior year in high school, and now a kind gesture he had made long ago had just saved my life's musical collection.

Dave dropped off my CDs a few hours later. Every last one of them was still in the case.

"I had been praying every night that you would find those CDs," my grandma told me.

"Really?" I said. "What about my clothes, Grandma? Those are still missing."

"I didn't pray for those to be returned," she said.

"Why not?"

"Well, if you got your clothes back, would you really want to wear them again, not knowing where they'd been?"

Hadn't I bought them from the Goodwill in the first place, not knowing where they'd been?

But I had no reason to complain. Things were looking up.

"It's a direct answer to prayer," my grandma said.

Because I had spent the night with my grandparents on a weekly basis growing up, they played a big role in raising me. My grandpa didn't mind when we ate tomatoes and rhubarb straight from his backyard garden or when we got into the Dr Peppers he kept in his garage refrigerator. My grandma took my cousins and me to amusement parks and swimming pools and on long bike rides to Dairy Queen. She helped us catch fireflies to put in a jar on our bedroom nightstands. She also prayed with us each night as she tucked us in to the tune of the little, enchanting buzzing lights. On those nights, I never doubted the validity of prayer.

An elementary school teacher once told me, "Nothing is 'just a coincidence'; everything is a God-incident." But I'm not sure if she was aware of the Law of Large Numbers, which says that since there are six billion people on earth, something that seems like it has a million-in-one chance of occurring will actually occur quite frequently—because in a large population, many odd coincidences are, in fact, *likely* to happen. I had always been a little confused when people labeled those odd coincidences "answers to prayer."

The day had finally arrived. Rachel and I prepared to go to work for the first time in months.

"Isn't it so ironic, the similarities between me and you and Lainey and Vickie?" Rachel asked me.

"Who are Lainey and Vickie?" I asked.

"They're only the main characters from your favorite movie ever."

As soon as I realized that Lainey and Vickie were the characters played by Winona Ryder and Janeane Garofalo in *Reality Bites*, I told Rachel it was most certainly *not* my favorite movie ever.

"It doesn't even make my top twenty-five," I said. "And, by the way, you really should use the actresses' real names rather than their characters' names when referencing them in casual conversation like that." Rachel countered by accusing me of hypocrisy with regard to a certain WB drama.

"Okay," I conceded. "I did *occasionally* reference Dawson, Joey, and Pacey by their first names ... but that was years ago."

In the past, I hadn't been afraid to embrace the lack of maturity and intelligence attributed to all *Dawson's Creek* fans. Without embarrassment, I would yell to Rachel, "I am *so* irritated with Joey! What's wrong with her? Why is she *still* thinking about Dawson?" (At least I had the brains to root for Pacey.)

"My point is," Rachel continued, "you and I are a lot like the two main characters on *Reality Bites*."

"How do you figure?" I asked.

"Well, first we couldn't find jobs after college, and we were lost and clueless and running out of money. Now we finally have jobs, but they're crap jobs. And I'm going to be working at the Gap just like Vickie, oh, whoops, I mean *Janeane* ... and you ..."

"I'm *what*?" I asked. "How are you going to compare me to Winona? Have you ever seen me shoplift?"

"No, but you do look a little bit like her," Rachel said.

Rachel was reaching. The only time in my life that I may have looked a little like Winona was in college, after I cut off all but two inches of my hair. I had hoped to look trendy and cool with super-short hair, but I didn't. I think people told me, "You look *just* like Winona" to distract me from the fact that I *really* looked like JFK Jr. My hair had since grown out.

With Rachel and I finally entering the working world, "reality bites" gave way to "reality mildly sucks." I didn't know which direction I was going with my life, but at least I was moving. I felt like I owed that to Dr. Porter's speech and our walk to his imaginary Possibility Place.

THREE

"Association with the spiritually immature is always painful
like association with an enemy.
Association with the wise is pleasant
like the coming together of relatives."
—Buddha

"Well, if it isn't the Dunkin' Donuts chick ..." Hunter was the first of my fellow servers to greet me at Paronelli's. The cab drivers had forewarned Rachel and me that everyone in Lincoln Park knew everyone else's business, but only after I started work at Paronelli's Pasta did I believe them.

Hunter was tall, maybe pushing six foot six. But apart from his height, he was about as nondescript as a twentysomething guy could be. He was one of those guys who would look ten times better if he put into practice some basic grooming measures—most notably, adding gel to his shaggy, unkempt head of hair.

Hunter always wore black pants that were much too short for his long legs, and they regularly exposed his white socks. He also wore a studded dog collar with matching belt and bracelet. Hunter told customers he graduated from the School of Rock. His favorite shirt read, "Debauchery is Life."

Hunter's sense of humor was his most redeemable quality. He was unusually witty, although highly sardonic. It was this characteristic that made him stand out in his improv class at Second City. Most students at the renowned comedy school were chasing *Saturday Night Live* pipe dreams, but Hunter was one of the few who actually had a chance of making it big.

I had been to see Hunter's Second City improv group, even though the show, for whatever reason, didn't start until one thirty in the morning. It was musical improv, which meant that every few minutes a pianist would strike up a melody, and the group would be forced to instantaneously turn their dialogue into a musical number, with both singing and dancing. Hunter always received the loudest applause. His delivery was seamless, and he stole the show.

Perhaps Hunter's capacity for greatness was the driving force behind his superiority complex. He acted like he was more intelligent, funny, and talented than everyone he knew. Because of this, there was a minute undercurrent of tension each time he entered a room. While in his presence, people experienced general feelings of inferiority, coupled with thoughts like "Who does this gangly punk idiot think he is?" I watched many people kowtow to Hunter out of fear—fear of becoming a new brunt for his jokes and fear of being permanently exiled from his far-reaching social network.

Jordan was Hunter's best friend and roommate, as well as a fellow Paronelli's server. The two were in a semi-popular, local punk band called Sidewalks in Hell. I heard their female fans drooled mercilessly over them, although I couldn't quite figure out why. It was easy to recognize the SIH groupies when they stopped by Paronelli's for pre-show beers and flirt sessions with the band's lead singer and bassist (Hunter and Jordan, respectively). With their goth garb and customary body piercings, the groupies were a stark contrast to the

Trixies. The groupies wore dark lipstick and had short hair dyed a rainbow of colors, extending out in every direction thanks to strong pomade. It was like they were begging for people to pinch their cheeks and gush, "You anti-establishment rebel, you!"

Most of Hunter and Jordan's friends lived in Wicker Park or Bucktown, where their dissident spirits had no trouble blending in. Hunter and Jordan stuck it out in Lincoln Park so they could be closer to work, even though they were obvious misfits in the culture they were trying to counter. Their overall attempts to oppose convention were painfully unoriginal, though, and the end result was a shelf full of books by Vonnegut, Bukowski, and Sedaris; a DVD collection of flicks such as *Donnie Darko*, *Reservoir Dogs*, and *Spinal Tap*; and a deep respect for the band The Clash. The bottom line was that they tried just a little *too* hard to convince the population at large that they were deeply disturbed.

Paronelli's Pasta, like most other Lincoln Park businesses, was long and narrow, its depth making up for its lack of width. There were floor-to-ceiling windows along the front, with glass panes that could easily slide open in warmer weather.

There was a long wooden bar down the center of the restaurant and a few high-top tables in front by the windows and in back by the wine cellar. The exposed brick walls were adorned with the standard Italian eatery decor, including long-necked bottles of oils, herbs, and spices placed on intermittent shelves. Low-watt bulbs hanging from the ceiling provided dim lighting.

Paronelli's customers had several entertainment options. Televisions mounted over either end of the bar were provided for viewing pleasure, and if nothing good was on television, patrons could watch the cooks prepare their food, as the kitchen was behind the bar, in full view of the customers. This open-kitchen feature enabled cook/diner interaction and gave the restaurant a more personal feel.

Hunter and I worked together every Friday and Saturday night.

"I'm clocking in now!" Hunter announced, in a voice much louder than usual. He followed it up with his trademark obnoxious evil cackle. Most Paronelli's customers were used to it and ignored him.

"Isn't that evil cackle number two for you already tonight?" I asked. "Want to tell me what's going on?"

"Our plan is brilliant, I tell you, brilliant!" Hunter was rubbing his hands together like a mad scientist.

He explained that he and Jordan were trying a new experiment called "never clocking out." They were staying clocked in twenty-four hours a day, seven days a week, and so far our less-than-lucid manager Brad didn't have a clue.

"We are genius," Hunter said. "I've been 'working' now for ten days straight."

"Good luck with that," I said, slightly irked because I knew only Hunter could get away with such a stunt. He was the lone Paronelli's server ever to get fired and then rehired, not once but twice.

"Are you coming to our show tonight?" Hunter asked. Sidewalks in Hell had a biweekly gig at some no-name bar up north in Rogers Park. "If you're lucky, maybe I'll give you a shout-out from the stage," Hunter said.

"You really think the ultimate incentive for me to come to your show is you, with loads of black eyeliner on, shouting my name from the beer-soaked stage of a dingy dive bar?" I asked.

"So you heard about my penchant for black liquid eyeliner?" Hunter *would* use the word "penchant."

I told him I had heard about both his eyeliner *and* how he got so drunk at each show that he could never remember which groupie he had slept with afterward.

"If you want, I could shout your name and then say ..." Hunter threw up a fist. "She's post-college! She's trying to figure out what to do with her life! So she's doing the craaaazy big-city thang!" Hunter loved to mock me and everyone else around him.

"Shut up." It was all I could muster for a swift comeback.

"How are you any different than me?" I asked. "You're what ... all of two years out of college?"

"Make that three," Hunter said, holding three fingers about two inches from my eyes. "And the main difference between you and me is that *I get it.* You're still naïve enough to think there's something else out there better than this."

The arrogant look in his eye made me think he was about to start cackling a third time.

"By the way," I said, "you just made up my mind for me. I'm not going to your show."

"You'll be there," he said confidently.

Hunter called it. I was weak, and I was sick of Paronelli's employees telling me, "You *have* to go to a Sidewalks in Hell show." Plus, I figured there was never anything wrong with a little rock 'n' roll.

But Sidewalks in Hell *wasn't* a little rock 'n' roll. Hunter didn't sing, he screamed. Deafening screams, mostly about casual sex and drugs. His eyes were rimmed in too much black eyeliner, as promised. Meanwhile, Jordan's eyes were half-closed, as though he was ready to pass out at any moment. I could tell Jordan was struggling just to keep his fingers moving across the strings of his bass guitar.

Hunter had on a tight black T-shirt that read "The Devil Gets a Bad Rap." He also wore his usual studded accessories and a pair of disgusting tapered jeans—disgusting simply because they were tapered. He was slamming his body against the stage walls and the equipment. He was flailing around in ways I didn't know were possible. The look in his eyes was enough to warrant a call for a priest and holy water. But although Hunter looked both possessed and insane, he mostly just looked like your average wasted lead singer of a rock band.

Instead of giving me a shout-out, Hunter gave one to "Chrissy Cocaine" and "Matty Meth," two friends who were problematic in the mosh pit. They were not abiding by any mosh pit rules of engagement, throwing punches randomly into the crowd. Rachel, who had graciously accompanied me to the show, got shoved into the mosh pit by an obese, tattooed, *shirtless* man, and I dove in to rescue her from the likes of Chrissy and Matty.

Everyone everywhere looked angry. But I couldn't blame them— the concert made me angry. I have always credited musicians with having one of the most powerful positions on earth. They create the soundtrack that the rest of us live our lives to. They develop melodies and lyrics that can control the way we feel. And the masses memorize and internalize their favorite songs. I thought these facts might cause musicians to come to the creative table with humility and respect for the incredible task they're given. Yet Hunter and Jordan had spent hours writing crass songs that served no purpose other than to generate additional angst in already-tormented people nicknamed for their drug of choice.

While I stood there listening to Sidewalks in Hell, a strange vision lessened my anger. I imagined I was at a barn dance on a Friday night in some small town in the country. I was dancing to songs by Garth Brooks and George Strait, songs that left me with something of redeeming value rather than a vivid reminder of man's vileness. I had never been anywhere near a barn in my life, and I had definitely never lived in the country, but at that moment, the thought of it brought me strange comfort.

In the country, I would be able to see the horizon-to-horizon expanse of sky. I rarely caught a glimpse of the sky in a city full of tall buildings. I never saw the sun set or the diamond stars dotting the veil of night. After I watched Hunter sing/scream for a while, I wondered if it was easier for city dwellers to become godless because they could potentially live for years without viewing the entire vastness of the blue sky.

As the show labored on, my craving for the country intensified. I wanted to be in the little towns I had visited with friends in college. Towns like Mount Vernon, Missouri, a city famous for its annual "Apple Butter Makin' Days" festival. Or Hartville, Missouri, which had a Christmas parade that went up Main Street, turned around, and came back down so everyone could watch twice. After the parade, the entire town gathered at the high school gymnasium to sing Christmas carols and listen to the Christmas story read aloud. It was in Hartville that I first went frog giggin' and snipe hunting. It was also there that I caught an eight-pound bass, which sealed my victory in a fishing contest between my friend Jason and me (our competitive spirits carried well beyond the campus library).

I longed for Orange City, Iowa, where the annual tulip festival wasn't complete without little Dutch boys in wooden shoes dumping buckets of water on the already spotless streets so that the women walking behind them could sweep it up with their brooms. I wanted to be in Van Buren, Arkansas, where I learned how to shoot a rifle and build a campfire, and just missed seeing a grizzly bear in the mountains because my friend Paul had yelled, "Look! It's a bear!" one second too late.

Hunter would have laughed at me for days had I described these small towns to him. But maybe that was the point. Those places were somehow the opposite of Hunter. And in a dark bar full of unrest, I longed for rest. I wanted to see cornfields, hay bales, and grazing cattle. I wanted to lie again by the lake on the rooftop of my friend's car, studying the different shades of blue at dusk while listening to the croaking frogs and the song "I Hope You Dance" playing softly on the car radio.

Hunter's voice cut through my fantasies of old red barns and big farmhouses as he shouted to the crowd, "Which one of you ladies is coming home with me tonight?" The girls went wild. He then spouted some obscenities, and the band staggered offstage. Thankfully, there was no encore.

Jordan approached Rachel and me a few minutes after the show was over. "I didn't want to be the jerk who didn't come over and say hi to you guys," he said.

"So now you're the jerk who did?" Rachel asked.

Jordan kept rubbing his barely open eyes with his palms. "Remember the other day when you asked me if I was interested in you?" he asked. He was directing his question at Rachel, but he must have mistaken her for someone else.

"Jordan, you've only met Rachel one time at the restaurant," I said. "You must be thinking of a different girl."

"Well, I'm not interested in you," Jordan said, speaking again to Rachel.

Rachel laughed off the odd exchange and waved a hand in front of Jordan's face to check his reflexes.

"Jordan, she *never* asked you if you were interested in her," I said. "This is my *roommate* Rachel, and you've only met her once."

"Hey ... hey now ..." Jordan put his hands up defensively. "There's no need to get upset here. Just because I'm not interested in your roommate doesn't mean I'm giving up on finding someone ... I'm still checking things out ... keeping my eyes open for the right girl..."

"More like keeping your eyes half-shut," Rachel said.

Jordan flashed us a "rock 'n' roll" sign, extending his pinky and index finger, then stumbled away.

The whole conversation was as nonsensical and pointless as the concert had been.

Some researchers have concluded that the longer people live apart from their traditional family, the more likely it is that they will develop social entities to take its place. In a city, that social entity is sometimes called an urban family—a group comprised of friends of friends of friends, sometimes including neighborhood business owners and workers seen on a consistent basis. Since urban families obviously don't share a home, they spend time together in restaurants and bars—the modern meccas of the metropolis.

Paronelli's Pasta was a hub for these groups. So was the bar across the street from Paronelli's, not so aptly named The Bar Next Door. The head bartenders, Kyle and Scott, shared an apartment with Hunter and Jordan. Because the four had a combined loyal following of regulars that extended well beyond Lincoln Park proper into Lakeview, Wrigleyville, and Old Town (not to mention Hunter and Jordan's ties to Wicker Park and Bucktown), the four roommates had unparalleled social knowledge and networking abilities.

Therefore, if a Trixie thought a Chad working at a Lincoln Park bank was cute, she could come into Paronelli's or go to The Bar Next Door and ask one of the four guys if they knew anything about the cute banker. Between the four, someone usually knew the banker and could provide his stats.

Lincoln Park and the surrounding north-side neighborhoods were prime examples of places with high "clustering coefficients." A clustering coefficient is determined by taking the number of people who *actually* know each other in any given area, divided by the number of people who could *possibly* know each other. In a city where people walk everywhere, seeing the same faces over and over is inevitable.

For instance, the Paronelli's wait staff was already acquainted with most of my friends from Dunkin' Donuts. Ian and Paul, the garbage men, had been carting away Paronelli's trash for decades. They were occasionally given meals "on the house" in exchange for carting away more trash than allowed by city regulations. Apparently there were some dirty politics in waste management. My buddy Black Jesus had been frequently kicked out of Paronelli's for trying to warn diners of the upcoming November apocalypse while they were eating. Umer the taxi driver was one of Hunter's favorite weekly regulars and showed up to some of his improv shows. Even my old pal Damien from England came in for dinner every now and then. (Fortunately, he was sober and didn't remember me.)

Many nights when people entered the restaurant, I wanted to repeat the lyrics penned by Eddie Vedder: "I seem to recognize your face, haunting, familiar, yet I can't seem to place it." With many first-time customers, I had a strong feeling that I had seen them before. And the truth was, I probably had ... somewhere ... on the streets of the city.

There were certain regulars Hunter targeted as the brunt of his jokes. He said these quirky customers combined to create "The Goof Troop." According to Hunter, Tarrah was a charter member of The Goof Troop. She was an unassuming girl who claimed to be working nonstop on a top-secret government project funded by the University of Chicago. Tarrah said her project would change the world of information gathering, but that was the only information we could gather from her. Many servers (especially Hunter) were dubious about the veracity of her project and wondered if she might be crazy.

"That Tarrah girl is one of the more questionable freaks who comes in here," Hunter once told me while adjusting his dog collar.

I ran into Tarrah once on my night off. She was drinking a chai in Caribou Coffee and working on her "project" via laptop. We talked about the weather, her new haircut, and how Caribou makes the best chai. I thought nothing of our interaction, but from that night on, whenever Tarrah came into Paronelli's for dinner, she brought a cup of Caribou's chai for me. Her random acts of kindness were reason enough for me to rush to her defense whenever Hunter used her name to solicit laughter. He insisted her top-secret project was creating a deadly poison that could go undetected in a cup of hot chai.

"Don't knock Tarrah," I said. "Maybe she really is working on a project for the government."

"Yeah," Hunter said. "It's called Operation Goof Troop."

Hunter also mocked religion at every opportunity. He occasionally called me "the Jesus freak" because I rarely joined the Paronelli's crew at The Bar Next Door after work. I once received a voice mail from Hunter that said: "Hey, it's me, Hunter. Listen, I'm just calling because I was reading my Bible today, and it just really moved me ... I mean, seriously, it really rocked my world ... and usually I don't have this strong of a reaction after reading *fiction*. So anyway, give me a call sometime, and we'll pray about it together. Oh, and could you work for me this Friday? Come on ... think about it ... what would Jesus do? Peace."

One of the few nights I did join everyone at The Bar Next Door after my shift, I arrived just in time to hear Hunter rehashing all his reasons for not believing in God. He sounded like a high-school girl gossiping about the most popular girl in class, picking apart her every possible fault and flaw—who, truth be told, only criticized the girl because she could not *be* her.

I was annoyed that all the other servers were too intimidated to challenge Hunter.

"Okay, Hunter," I said. "If not God, how do you believe we got here?"

"You can't ask that question," he said. "You can't ask me, 'How did we get here?' if your implication is that God must have put us here."

"*This* had to all be caused by something ..." I said.

"That is so ignorant," Hunter said. "People who say the world has to have a first cause and then turn around and point to God as that first cause are not thinking. Their logic has already implied that God Himself must also have a first cause. So when they tell me, 'God doesn't have a first cause; He just always *was*,' it doesn't make any sense because they've shifted their logic to admit that some things don't have a first cause. If a person's willing to admit that some things don't have a first cause, why can't they concede that it may just as well be the world instead of God?"

I vaguely recalled reading about the kalam argument, which could have countered Hunter's first-cause rhetoric. Sadly, like most things I read, I only remembered the overall theme and could not articulate any specifics. "I thought that only something that begins to exist has to have a first cause," I said. "That would mean something that didn't have a beginning wouldn't need a first cause."

"Two words for you," Hunter said. "Quantum physics. Things can materialize in a vacuum."

"So you honestly think that everything on this planet came about by pure cosmic chance?" I asked.

"Don't go getting all sentimental on me about creative design and the intricate detail in the universe, blah blah blah ..." Hunter said. "I swear, people always want to run their mouths and give a Creator all the credit for the world's natural beauty. But suddenly they have nothing to say when they get asked who deserves the credit for the world's natural disasters. I mean, let's just look at this century alone ... in 1923, 100,000 people near Tokyo died in an earthquake. In 1931, flooding from the Yangtze River in China led to the death of three million people. In 1970, floods killed 300,000 people in Bangladesh, and meanwhile a snow avalanche killed 20,000 people in Peru. In 1976, an earthquake in China killed an estimated 655,000 people. In 1985, a volcano in Columbia killed 23,000 people. In 1990, a landslide in Iran killed 50,000 people ... do you want me to go on?" I said no. "In the Bible it talks about God causing earthquakes and famines and disease to punish people for their sins," Hunter said. "So why not give God some credit for all the natural disasters today since that seems to be His MO."

"Maybe they should," I said. I had heard most Christians explain natural disasters in scientific terms having nothing to do with God. The rare person who suggested that natural disasters might be God's way of getting our attention were dismissed as cold, callous, and rather absurd; most had never experienced tragedy themselves. However, maybe Hunter had a point. I remembered reading something in Jeremiah 5 where God said,

> Do you have no respect for Me? Why do you not tremble in My presence? I, the Lord, am the One who defines the ocean's sandy shoreline, an everlasting boundary that the waters cannot cross ... But My people have stubborn and rebellious hearts. They have turned against Me and have chosen to practice idolatry. They do not say from the heart, "Let us live in awe of the Lord our God" ... Among My people are wicked men ... Like a cage filled with birds, their homes are filled with evil plots. And the

result? Now they are great and rich. They are well fed and well groomed, and there is no limit to their wicked deeds ... Should I not avenge Myself against a nation such as this? (NLT)

"Can we talk about Christians specifically for a minute?" Hunter asked. He didn't wait for my reply. "Christians say that God is good and all-powerful, which would imply that He has the power to positively intervene in the world, but He doesn't. So how can He allow so much violence, war, genocide ... and epidemics like depression, AIDS, physical and sexual abuse of children ..."

"But you can't blame the sun for the darkness, can you?" I interrupted.

"I can, and I will," Hunter said. "If God can see all those things happening and could do something about them but doesn't, I have no interest in Him. And seriously, *why* would I want to be a Christian when all Christians do is talk about how they're miserable, worthless sinners? Nobody can be emotionally healthy and useful for the common good if he's a self-deprecating, introspective idiot. Not to mention how much time Christians waste passing on their dogmatic rules. Somehow they can't realize that constantly telling everyone what they *aren't* allowed to do doesn't mean people will stop being interested in doing those things. People will just become *more* intrigued with the 'forbidden' than they would have been otherwise."

I couldn't help thinking about Lao Tzu's wise words: "Law after law breeds a multitude of thieves. Therefore a sensible man says if I keep from commanding people, they behave themselves; if I keep from preaching at people, they improve themselves."

"I mean, come on," Hunter said. "No smoking, no drugs, no drinking, no cursing, no sex ... I broke every one of those rules in the last twenty-four hours. So do you think I'm going to hell?"

I certainly hoped not. Hunter might not exactly be a kindred spirit, but he was a funny and intelligent human being. If I even suggested that I believed in hell, the implication would be that the entire Paronelli's crew would likely end up there. But I couldn't blame our manager Brad for the fact that his good Catholic upbringing wasn't enough to sustain his faith after his "Christian" wife left him for another man. And I couldn't fault Abu, Paronelli's delivery guy, for dutifully following the faith of his mother who was raised in a country that was 99 percent Muslim.

"I don't know about hell," I said. "I've heard it explained that heaven is a display of God's mercy, and hell a display of His justice. Because God is perfect, He can't allow anything unclean into His presence. So if hell is, more than anything else, a separation from God, we all deserve the justice of hell. But a few are granted the mercy of heaven." Even as the words came out of my mouth, I recognized how silly they sounded.

"One problem," Hunter said. "The Bible doesn't just describe hell as a clean little 'separation from God.' The way Jesus talks about hell, with all its wailing and gnashing of teeth, just makes me sick. How could any respectable person say some people might end up in a fire pit for eternity? How can people who didn't have a choice in their own existence be made to suffer forever?"

I told Hunter I didn't know.

When I was young, Ryan, my ten-year-old embodiment of true love, asked a pastor, "Do people who don't know Jesus go to hell?" The pastor replied, "Unfortunately they do." At the time, Ryan didn't understand the word "unfortunately." He had only heard his mom use it in the following context: "Unfortunately, if you don't get your math homework done, you can't watch *Duck Tales*." For a few years he connected hell with an absence of cartoons.

I remember reading Angie Fenimore's book, *Beyond the Darkness*, about her near-death experience in hell. She said, "[In hell] men and women were wandering on a plane. They were completely self-absorbed, every one of them too caught up in his or her own misery to engage in any mental or emotional exchange." As she reached for more information, she said she felt tremendous disappointment. The possibilities for learning were endless, but there were no conduits for growth, like books. There was simply no knowledge to gain and no way to use it. She said the worst part was her growing sense of total aloneness. "Even hearing the brunt of someone's anger, however unpleasant, is a form of tangible connection. But in this empty world, where no connections could be made, the solitude was terrifying."

Then there was the question of heaven. If there was a heaven, I hoped it was similar to the movie *What Dreams May Come*—a compilation of all the sights, smells, food, people, places, and activities each person had grown to love while on earth.

In a discussion about heaven, there's always one character who feels the burning need to ask, "But what would we *do* for all of eternity?" I believe people who have the capacity to "become bored" are usually themselves boring people. If heaven is anything like earth, there will be more than enough to keep us busy ... going on African safaris, hiking through the Himalayas, bicycling through quaint villages in France, and swimming alongside humpback whales off the Atlantic coast. Maybe heaven will include nightly concerts at beautiful outdoor amphitheaters. Billions of people singing in unison conjured up images of celestial status. But somehow I doubted the concerts would involve harps, Latin hymns, or Gregorian chants; I imagined something more like the Boss playing an appropriate and otherworldly rendition of "The Rising."

After years of afterlife hypotheses, I finally consulted the Bible for its description of heaven. According to Revelation 21, heaven is not an ethereal idea; it is a literal city. It's a city that is 1,400 miles wide and 1,400 miles long. The city walls are 1,400 miles high and 200 feet thick, made from twelve precious stones including jasper, sapphire, emerald, and amethyst. There are twelve gates into the city, three on each side of the four walls. Each gate is made of a single pearl. The main street of the city is made from pure gold that looks like transparent glass.

Revelation 22 talks about a flowing, crystal-clear river running through the main street of the city and the tree of life, yielding an abundance of fruit. It says that the city doesn't need the sun or moon to shine because the glory of God gives it light. Apparently, God had to hang the sun to give light to the earth because He could not be there Himself. But in heaven, the light of God radiates magnificently through the jeweled walls. There is no evil, sadness, or confusion within the city; there is only goodness, happiness, and peace.

Plato believed that whenever we see something beautiful, good, or right on earth and feel that deep inner sense of appreciation and awe, it is because we are "remembering the Forms." We might be recalling the Form of Beauty, Truth, Goodness, or Virtue. Forms are the true reality that exists somewhere beyond the shadow of reality we experience here on earth, and we will always feel a pang of emotion whenever we see the Forms captured in our world.

Maybe fairytale-like surroundings that evoke our awe-filled silences are limited to just that ... fairy tales. Perhaps there is no wonder beyond. Or maybe every sunset and rainbow is trying to remind us that there is something more. Perhaps when we "ooh and ahh" over someone's new diamond ring, we do so because we've literally just experienced a tiny glimpse of heaven.

"The Christian God *might* exist," Hunter said. "Just like the thirty-three million Hindu gods *might* exist. But we have to be realistic and admit that religion is more than likely what we've thought it's been this whole time—just humanity's attempt to ease fear. People are afraid of the unknown, so they say, 'God has a plan.' People are worried they don't have a purpose, so they say, 'I was called to do this.' People are afraid of death, so they say, 'I'm going to heaven.' People hate that they can't control the world, so they pray, and suddenly they feel like they're 'working alongside God' with the power to help decide what happens in the universe."

Hunter turned his body so that some of the other servers sitting near us could hear him. "The bottom line is that Marx was right," he said. "There is no doubt in my mind that religion is nothing more than the opiate of the people."

That's what I got for going to The Bar.

FOUR

WHO IS JOHN GALT?

"Play, pleasures, mirth, and worldly joys,
be done with these and heed them not."
—Buddha

Just because Rachel and I had jobs didn't mean we were about to give up our leisurely days at Dunkin' Donuts. We spent our afternoons as we always had, lounging with our Mocha Blasts and chatting with the eclectic clientele. At five thirty in the evening, we would meander down the street a few blocks to our individual workplaces just in time for our six o'clock shifts to begin.

Tanner was new to the Dunkin' Donuts scene. He sported blond dreadlocks and red-rimmed spectacles. He was a student at the Art Institute downtown, and he gave us daily updates on how his semester art project was coming along. "You guys should stop by my apartment one of these days and check it out for yourselves," he said.

Forgetting names like Ted Bundy and John Wayne Gacy, we took him up on his offer and found his art project to be a geometric-shape study that wasn't quite as grand as he had painted it to be.

As Rachel and I stood up to leave Tanner's place, he said, "Would you mind if I read you something before you go?" Oblivious to the wary glances Rachel and I exchanged, Tanner pulled up a chair in front of us and sat down with a book of poetry in his hand. He cleared his throat, and when he began to read, he spoke in a voice at least three octaves higher than normal. "Friendship is sacred ..." he said in his brand-new voice. He went on to read a two-minute poem about the joys of friendship. When he finished, he closed the book and, in his normal voice, said, "The reason I asked if I could read you this today ... is so that you would understand that I plan on taking this new friendship with you girls seriously." We promptly made our exit.

We later learned that Tanner was a bit of a neighborhood legend. Five of my regulars at the restaurant told me Tanner had also invited them back to his apartment under a "semester art project" pretext. Rachel thought maybe Tanner just really needed some friends. I agreed that he might be a well-meaning guy, but I also told her it would take a lot for me to excuse his poetry performance.

I worked with Jordan, Hunter's best friend, every Tuesday night. The first day I met Jordan, he told me, "The one thing you need to know about me is that if I ever get to go to an AC/DC concert, I'll probably kill someone in the audience." He then threw up his infamous "rock 'n' roll" hand sign and contorted his features into the ugliest face imaginable, with his tongue dangling from the side of his mouth. Then he yelled, "That's how crazy I can get about AC/DC!" Nice to meet you, too.

Jordan was almost as tall as Hunter, but he took a little more pride in his presentation. His blond hair usually contained some gel or other product, and he had splurged on black socks. Jordan and a day server named Kelly had an on-again, off-again relationship—

on each time the band got close to signing with a label, off each time Kelly heard rumors about Jordan sleeping with the band's groupies. Jordan admitted he only went out with Kelly so he could tell people he was seeing a former *Playboy* model. Kelly had indeed modeled for the magazine, but most people who met her were surprised by her mouth full of metal braces and her four-foot-eleven frame—she easily could have passed as a twelve-year-old, were it not for one particular surgical enhancement. The miracle of airbrushing didn't seem to faze Jordan.

Jordan was eating crab-stuffed mushrooms before our shift, and I sat down next to him to mooch off his plate.

"Did you like our show?" he asked.

"Nope," I said. "I'm not into that whole scene."

"I told Hunter that wasn't your style," he said. "You're more of an Amy Grant-type girl."

I rerouted the conversation. "Your apartment is pretty sweet though."

Rachel and I had stopped by briefly for the "after-party," which consisted of a room full of uninteresting people who desperately needed to be in rehab.

"How much do you guys pay for that place?" I asked.

"I think rent's something like $5,600 a month," he said. "Then you've got utilities on top of that. But it's split up between me, Hunter, Scott, Kyle, Kenya, and Bria."

"Do I know Kenya and Bria?" I asked.

"I think you met Kenya at The Bar one night. She's not around much because she's always visiting her boyfriend in Milwaukee. I don't think you've ever met Bria."

"How do you know those girls?"

"They answered an ad we put in the paper."

"I can't get over how much you pay for rent," I said, eating Jordan's last mushroom. "We'd better get to work so you can start making some money to pay your bills."

"No rush ..." Jordan said, grinning. "I'm making money while I sleep, remember? I'm clocked in twenty-four/seven."

Waiting tables at Paronelli's Pasta was easy because the heart and soul of Paronelli's—the regulars—made it easy. Many times the cooks already knew what the regulars wanted before they opened their mouths to order. Either that, or the regulars would give their order directly to the cooks, eliminating the need for a server altogether— but still leaving a $5 tip for the meal. Since servers didn't have to work too hard then, we mostly shot the breeze, watched TV, and occasionally entered an order into the computer. We kept water glasses full and recommended specific wines with entrées.

Lincoln Park residents tipped an average of 20 to 25 percent, so if a server could accumulate a faithful group of regulars, he or she could count on a set amount of tip money coming in each month. This alleviated some of the stress that resulted from making a living based on other people's generosity. But amassing a faithful group of regulars wasn't easy. People requested servers less for their serving capabilities than for their up-to-date knowledge of neighborhood gossip.

"Pam's divorce will be final this week," Lance, one of my Tuesday night regulars, said. "Somebody should tell Brad about it."

Lance had been trying to set up Pam and Brad for months.

"Lance, give up the dream," I said. "It's common knowledge that Pam is interested in you, not Brad."

"Well, I can tell you *that's* not happening," Lance said.

Pam was a regular who drank two glasses of Shiraz each night before her dinner while perusing the *New York Times*. She was very intelligent, completing the *Times* crossword puzzle in full each night. But brains didn't interest Lance. He had recently been featured on *Oprah* as one of America's fifty most eligible bachelors over fifty. Since his fifty minutes of fame, he had become very picky about whom he would and would not date.

"That's so sad about Pam's divorce," I said, setting down Lance's usual iced tea/no lemon in front of him.

"Pam's divorce is a good thing," Lance said. "Her husband worked all the time. He was never around."

"But don't they have three kids still at home?" I asked.

"So what if they have kids?" Lance said. "Don't go getting all religious on me now, talking about the evils of divorce."

"It has nothing to do with religion," I said. "It has to do with common sense, based on documented research."

"What research?" Lance asked.

"Research shows that children from divorced homes are more than twice as likely as those raised in intact two-parent homes to suffer from serious psychiatric disorders—especially depression, suicide or suicide attempt, and alcohol addiction." I wasn't sure if Lance wanted me to go on, but I did anyway. "Girls from divorced homes are three times more likely to get addicted to drugs, and boys are four times more likely."

"Oh, lighten up," Lance said. "Didn't college teach you there's a statistic to prove anything?"

"I just recited the results from a study of all children in Sweden ... that's more than one million kids," I said. "That's no small statistic."

"I'll believe it when I see it," Lance said.

"All I'm saying is that children from divorced homes—where there was no abuse or infidelity—are being taught a terrible message," I said. "They're learning that when a person gets angry enough or bored enough with another person, it's okay to terminate that relationship. A child who subconsciously internalizes that message will never feel totally safe in any relationship again. The fact that 'mommy and daddy just don't love each other anymore' makes the child feel like a leftover byproduct of a family that failed. Divorce teaches kids there's really no such thing as unconditional love."

"Wow, are you finished yet?" Lance asked, looking genuinely annoyed. "You're in the wrong business. Why don't you stop waiting tables and become a spokesperson for the Christian coalition?" It was strange how using deductive logic kept earning me the title of "religious fanatic."

"I think Pam's kids will be just fine," Lance continued. "Pam's a good mom."

"I'm not saying Pam's not a good mom," I said. "But there will be a lot of factors she can't control after the divorce that might limit how 'good of a mom' she can be. When you're trying to put your own life back together—with personal, emotional, and financial issues—it gets harder to devote a lot of time and energy to your kids."

"She'll figure it out," Lance said. "By the way, is Chris here?" It was a sly way to change the subject. He was looking for Chris Paronelli.

"Lance, let's pretend that Paronelli's is Middle-earth," I said. "You do realize that Chris is Saron, right?"

Lance laughed. "Hey, that's my buddy you're talking about."

"He's not here," I said. "I'll go tell Mario to get your food ready though. Do you want your garlic bread today?" Lance got a plate of garlic bread before every meal, but I had recently heard him mention some type of diet to Brad. I thought I would ask, just in case he was on Atkins.

"No garlic bread today, but I'll have it tomorrow," he said.

Was there some type of part-time Atkins diet I wasn't aware of?

One of Jordan's regulars was a man Hunter labeled the president of The Goof Troop and also nicknamed the "Sleeveless Psycho," or just Psycho for short. Psycho had a kind of Kenny Chesney approach to clothing; he dressed as though shirts with sleeves did not exist. Psycho only came to Paronelli's during Cubs games. The restaurant broadcast every Cubs game on TV and got busy during home games since Wrigley Field was less than a mile away. The crowds, however, never deterred Psycho.

Psycho earned his moniker years ago when Jordan noticed that each time Sammy Sosa stepped up to the plate, Psycho started talking *to* Sammy through the television, and not in an excited fan type of way.

"Sammy, you've *got* to wait for my signal," he would say. "You haven't been working with me lately, and I don't like your attitude. You can't go it alone. You need my help with this pitcher. He's a hard one to read. So start paying some attention to my calls, and I'll lead you through it."

Years ago Brad asked Mr. Paronelli if he could ban Psycho from eating at Paronelli's because his unnecessary monologues were disturbing other customers. Mr. Paronelli's reply was, "Bad marketing is good marketing. I don't care if the guy scares off a couple Trixies—we get *more* people coming into this restaurant just because they've heard about the 'guy who talks to Sammy Sosa,' and they want to see him live. That Psycho guy has always been good for business. Case closed." Hence, the Sleeveless Psycho became an integral piece of Paronelli's Pasta's business strategy.

Each time Psycho came in to eat, he ordered the same thing, using precisely the same words and voice intonation: "Um, yeah [two-second pause] I think this time I'll order the rigatoni, plain with a little meat sauce on the side ... and a water to drink."

Then one night—perhaps it was a full moon or perhaps the

Cubs were actually getting close to the World Series ... we couldn't be sure what prompted a change in the cosmic balance—Psycho stunned us all with his order. Psycho said to Jordan, "Um, yeah [two-second pause] I think this time I'll order the rigatoni, plain with a little meat sauce on the side ... and a *Heineken* to drink." The restaurant staff flew into an uproar. Psycho had ordered a Heineken instead of water! Had he substituted his water for a Coke or an iced tea, the whole experience may not have been so jarring, but a Heineken! It was the biggest news of the night, if not the week. Jordan drew a picture of Psycho and hung it in the office. The speech bubble proclaimed, "I'll take a Heineken," and the title read: "Just when you think you know someone ..."

Jordan was a big fan of philosopher Ayn Rand. Hunter told me that Jordan wouldn't speak to him for days after he refused to name their band Who is John Galt?, a line made famous in Ayn Rand's book *Atlas Shrugged*.

Like Rand, Jordan believed only in objective reality, which sounds basic but really isn't. By believing in objective reality, a person forfeits all spirituality because anything supernatural suggests there is more to existence than what meets the eye. Objectivists believe it is foolish to think more exists than what actually does. "Things are what they are, and wishing there is a spiritual realm we can't see doesn't make that realm exist," Jordan said.

When business was slow, Jordan presented object lessons on Objectivism for anyone who'd listen.

"See this table?" He hit a table with his fist. "This table exists, right? You and I know that anything we see exists in reality, so because we can see this table, we know it exists."

"Sure ..." I said unenthusiastically.

"Let's label this table A," he said. "Now would you agree that A is A, and will always be A?" I nodded. "Then if A is all that exists right here in this space, can you tell me why people keep asking if there's a B?" Jordan said.

"I would ask about B because A is clearly made by a carpenter who used the wood from a tree," I said.

"You aren't getting it," Jordan said. "I'm talking about just this right here ... just A ... just the table."

I looked again at the table. "I guess I don't get it then," I said.

"Someone who says that what he sees in the universe must come from a creator isn't in touch with reality. That person has insisted on jumping beyond the world that exists into a silly idea that people developed over time, which has no basis in reality. The concept of a God is ludicrous. Some creative people just threw together the good characteristics of man and added a few irrational characteristics that have never been seen in reality—like omniscience and omnipresence—and poof, the concept of God was born."

"So maybe no one can prove there's a God," I said. "But you can't prove that there *isn't* a God."

"See, now you're talking about proving or disproving something that is outside our cognitive responsibility to know with a rational mind," he said. "Before you can ask me a question about anything, I first have to know that the thing you're asking me about is something. If it is not something I can see in reality, your question isn't valid because there is nothing to be said about it. If someone asks me, 'Is there a God?' I can't say, 'I don't know,' because that implies I haven't studied the evidence for or against it, and maybe someday, if I studied hard enough, I could know. But there is no evidence to be studied because we are in a physical reality where no God exists. So your question to me is irrelevant because it cannot be cognitively processed."

"So you're saying that nothing else exists except what we can see?" I asked.

"Yeah," Jordan said. "There's nothing mysterious or unknowable about the universe. What is here now is all that we can ever know. Ultimate truth is just the recognition of reality."

"But isn't each man's recognition of reality different?" I asked. "Is each man just supposed to live by his own truth and his own personal morality code?"

"Yes," he said. "But not in the way you're thinking. Ayn Rand taught that man is a rational being. He will live by a code of morals no matter what, because it's rational to do so. So just because someone embraces the truth of reality doesn't mean that person is going to live an immoral life. It's ignorant to try to link human morality to a higher power. Morality is good for the whole of humanity. It has nothing to do with God. Therefore, a godless man can and often will practice good morality."

I smirked, and Jordan read my mind. "The fact that I've slept with half of Chicago doesn't negate what I just said."

"It doesn't?" I asked.

"No, because I'm still working on bringing my mind into harmony with reality and accepting that what is here now is all that I can know. Once I do this *completely*, I will be a fully rational being. And people who are fully rational are always moral."

The expression on my face must still have been one of confusion.

"Try to follow me," Jordan said. "Each individual can think and reason. His reasoning affects his emotions, and his emotions affect his actions. As long as I pay attention to what I'm thinking, I will slowly become more and more rational. I will eventually use my rationality to determine my own character and life."

"So you're saying that each man creates his own destiny using his thoughts?" I asked.

"Yeah," Jordan said. "Man is essentially self-created and self-directed. When a man is responsible for what he thinks, he is responsible for all the consequences that come from his thoughts.

In that sense, he really is a self-made soul. If you study up on Objectivist ethics, you'll start to understand what I'm talking about."

"I would think somebody was really pompous if he told me he was 'self-made,'" I said.

"That's because you don't understand egoism yet," he said. "One of the greatest virtues taught in Objectivism is egoism—the pursuit of self-interest or the policy of selfishness. Egoism means that it's each man's moral obligation to achieve his own self-interest. A man *should* be selfish because only he is the beneficiary of his own actions. Altruistic men who go around self-sacrificing for others need to believe their work serves others, whether it does or not. They also need to believe their motivation is for the good of others, whether it is or not. An Objectivist admits that all words and actions of man have some element of selfishness, and that that is not only okay but good."

I thought about what Jordan believed and the age-old debate about selfishness. *Is* man capable of doing anything that doesn't have even the slightest selfish motive? People who give to charity are able to maintain their own comforts, status, and position while giving of their excess and feeling better about themselves. Parents who help their children financially usually have their children's best interests in mind, but they have the added interest of not wanting to see their children fail because it might affect others in the family. A woman who is extremely involved in a church might want to help others, but she probably also wants to perpetuate the feeling that she is important and needed by other people. We don't want people we love to die because our lives would be miserable without them.

So is there anything we think or do that is purely out of concern for another? Or are we acting on our own behalf even during our most altruistic moments? And does it really matter either way? Isn't the point to make a good choice in the moment, regardless of the complex motives that may lie beneath the surface?

Jordan's Objectivist viewpoint as it related to welfare led to some heated debates with our endless supply of liberal regulars. Jordan thought it was pointless for a nation to give a blank check (funded by other people's hard work) to a lost cause. He said, "If a kid struggles hard to get through school and, after he gets out, has to pay taxes to help fund government dropout programs, what does that tell him about ambition and scholastic achievement? Or if a couple saves up for years to buy their first home, but the couple on the other side of town can live rent-free thanks to a public housing program, what does that tell the first couple about hard work and financial discretion?"

Lance and Brad berated Jordan one day for taking such a politically incorrect stance, but their anger only fueled Jordan's fire.

Jordan had studied art and design in college until he became passionate about objectivism and decided that today's visual arts communicate nothing. "They are ruled by the principle of distortion," he said. "They're distortions of perspective, space, shape, color, and especially the human figure. These distortions pursue us everywhere we go, from ads to exhibits at an art gallery. The purpose of these distortions is to make us doubt the evidence of our senses that tells us all art is nothing like reality. Our society wants us to doubt the sanity of our own minds so it they can control them."

I imagined my ex Michael Vaughn would get along splendidly with Jordan.

After deciding not to pursue art in college, Jordan switched his major to philosophy. He graduated with the ability to argue Objectivism any time and any place, but he was now limited to the confines of a place that smelled like fresh garlic and sun-dried tomatoes. The high level of education among the people I knew in the Chicago service industries astounded me. Ironic as it was, Hunter had a communications degree. Another server named Nola was working toward her master of psychology, while a server named Haley just graduated with a BS in marketing. Kyle from The Bar Next Door had a BA in creative writing, and his sidekick Scott had a master of business. The fact that so many people were in the same position I was gave me a great degree of comfort. We were all educated up with nowhere to go, so we waited on people and waited for a better opportunity to come along.

"Come over to The Bar tonight, and I'll try to better explain Objectivist ethics," Jordan said, as the dinner rush began. "You know I'm better at explaining all this stuff after I've had a few shots."

Jordan was the biggest bar fly of the entire Paronelli's crew. He said if he couldn't listen to AC/DC while drinking, he would start to "lose it," which is why Jordan had drunk at The Bar Next Door every night since Kyle had given him permission to put some of his burned AC/DC mixes on the jukebox.

"I'm not going to The Bar tonight," I said. "I'm picking up a day shift tomorrow, and I need to get to bed early."

"You Mormons are so lame, I swear," he said.

FIVE

TRIXIE STICKS

"The only true beauty is the beauty of the heart."
—Rumi

There had been an infiltration. Two Chads were standing in line at Dunkin' Donuts, and Rachel and I had no choice but to stand behind them.

Rachel said the shorter Chad reminded her of her ex-boyfriend Matt Smith. Whenever I remembered Matt, the word "cardboard" popped into my head because Rachel had once described him as being "so dull that it seemed like he was trying to impersonate cardboard"—an interesting analogy, I thought. Matt had a certain lack of variety in his life that irritated Rachel. She cringed when they went to Einstein Bros. Bagels and Matt ordered a plain bagel with regular cream cheese. She marveled when they went to Baskin-Robbins and Matt asked for just one scoop of vanilla ice cream in a sugar-free cone. At Gino's Pizza, Matt ordered plain old cheese pizza, and whenever they ate at a steakhouse, Matt requested his steak be cooked "medium." Matt's average-joe persona didn't cut it, so Rachel cut it off.

The Matt look-alike turned and noticed us in line. "How you doin'?" was his choice for a brilliant, one-of-a-kind opener.

The other Chad followed it up with "Can we get you ladies' names and numbers?"

"I'm kind of seeing someone," Rachel said. "But my roommate's single, and she'd probably love to give you her number."

"It's true," I said before rattling off Rachel's cell phone number.

Haley was an outgoing Trixie from Nebraska. She was sugary sweet in her speech, throwing around "babe" and "hon" and other terms of endearment when talking with customers. She carried a big bag that boasted her sorority letters and contained a mini MAC makeup studio for touchups during her shifts. Haley hoped to earn better tips by wearing glam makeup, dangling earrings, and glitter on her collarbone.

Haley told me, "I don't try to hide the fact that I'm materialistic and shallow. I will *only* marry a man who's filthy rich. Money is so much more important than love, and any girl who says it's not is lying." Haley was known for her 106 pairs of shoes and her 102-pound frame that screamed eating disorder. She denied all accusations. Mark told me there was an ongoing game at the restaurant (unbeknownst to Haley) called the "try to get Haley to eat something" game. There was no winner to date.

Haley subscribed to *Cosmopolitan* and *Glamour*, and she brought them to work so she could pore over the diet and fashion articles and stare wistfully at the glossy ads whenever business was slow.

"Look at this girl." Haley shoved a page of *Cosmo* in my face as I filled up a water glass. "This girl's stomach is so flat ... how does she do it? I've tried everything."

I refused to engage Haley in such an antiquated ritual. I would not dance the dance of "I look so fat in this ..." "No you don't! You're soooo thin." "No, *you're* so thin. I look huge."

Hunter had said it best: Haley was starving for attention.

The art director of a very well-known magazine once told a reporter, "No picture of any woman in any magazine ever goes in unretouched." But even if Haley knew that, it wouldn't make an ounce of difference. She wanted to look like those pictures even if they were just illusions. She was going to look like them if it killed her. And with 150,000 women dying of anorexia each year, it just might. I had heard there were 3.5 million anorexic and bulimic women in the UK alone, and 78 percent of all girls under age eighteen report feeling "dissatisfied" with their body. Those numbers should be reason enough for women to stop supporting the lies Haley eagerly bought into. Why couldn't she grasp that advertisers *had* to lower women's self-esteem in order to create a need for their products? That was their job. If the dieting industry couldn't create the need to be thin, they would lose their market share of $33 billion a year. If the anti-aging industry couldn't ensure that every model in her sixties would be retouched to look forty-five (a standard technique), they might not be able to earn their usual $20 billion per year. The goal was to bombard women at every turn, and they had been successful, with the average woman now viewing four hundred to six hundred advertisements each day.

I wanted to dismiss Haley as just another easily manipulated casualty of an economically driven world, but in rare moments, I caught a glimpse of something more to her—her true beauty shining through. Like when she made one of her classic shockingly honest comments and blushed and giggled, or when she looked at me with eyes of genuine gratefulness, saying, "Thank you for accepting me as I am." But then the moment would pass as Haley returned to talking about the joys of couture.

Haley and I didn't get along at first. Thanks to her steady diet of women's magazines in place of actual food, her social abilities had been stunted because she saw all unknown women as her adversaries. I refused to fall prey to her female cattiness, and I didn't want every Wednesday night to be miserable for both of us, so I used a fail-proof tactic to win Haley over: I bought her a pair of dangling earrings from a Lincoln Park boutique and told her, "I saw these and thought of you."

Haley not only adored me from that moment on, but also deemed me her sole confidant with regard to her trials and tribulations with Jackson, a Chad she'd been seeing for the past year.

Jackson worked downtown as a stockbroker, minding other people's stocks while neglecting his own. Like most Chads, his dad had helped him land an amazing job that gave him instant status beyond his years, but his title was definitely not an indicator of his maturity.

"You will not believe what Jackson did the other night," Haley said between sips of coffee. Haley satisfied any oral fixation she had during work with cup after cup of black coffee.

"What'd he do?" I asked.

"So we were at John Barleycorn's, and he starts flirting with Amy right in front of me," Haley said.

Each time I told Haley to dump Jackson, she agreed wholeheartedly with me that she should move on. But the next time she was drunk or lonely, my advice had little bearing. Haley reminded me of the typical woman who called the Dr. Laura radio show. After talking about all the horrendous things her boyfriend had done, the woman would finish by asking Dr. Laura, "So, should I stay with him?" Dr. Laura, ever the voice of sanity, would remind her—often with well-deserved harshness—that the problem was not the guy; it was the fact that the woman was screwed up enough to ask the question. Until Haley respected herself enough to believe she deserved someone better than Jackson, my comments would continue to fall on deaf ears. But at least those deaf ears would look good in new dangling earrings.

Even though some of the Paronelli's regulars were characters fit for a Christopher Guest movie, the boring but honest truth was that most regulars were just standard Trixies and Chads. They were high-maintenance, but at least they left high tips to compensate.

With *Sex and the City* in between seasons, Wednesdays became the most popular night for Trixie clientele since the restaurant TVs broadcast *The Bachelor*. The girls watched the show while daintily picking at spinach salads and sipping glasses of Pinot Grigio. They swooned over the brainless bachelor, since some of them had at least that much in common with him.

By six thirty, every chair and barstool in the restaurant displayed a perfectly coiffed female—blondes with twists of lowlights, brunettes with splashes of highlights, and more blondes straight up.

A typical conversation during those hours sounded like this:

"Can you *believe* I accidentally grabbed my black Kate Spade purse instead of my navy blue one! I am *so* mismatched right now. I seriously feel like everyone's staring at me!"

"If anyone's staring at you, it's because you're standing next to me, and I look like such a cow in these pants."

"We need a bottle of Pinot in a bucket of ice," one Trixie requested, tapping a freshly manicured French tip on the high wooden table. "And make sure the bruschetta comes out *before* the salad. Do *not* bring it out *with* the salad. Oh, and I noticed that the TV isn't turned to ABC yet for *The Bachelor*. Could you make sure that gets taken care of? Thanks." She flashed a condescending smile of straight, bleached-white teeth.

"It's her bachelorette party!" another girl shouted to a table of Chads. At least three nights a week, a veiled Trixie in a "suck for a buck" shirt stumbled into Paronelli's, followed by her tribe of friends. The objective observer might think Trixies spent all their free time throwing and attending bachelorette parties. I guess with daddy paying for law school, a $450,000 condo, and a new Jetta, there wasn't much else to do. And studying might quickly become overwhelming with words like "jurisprudence" to pronounce.

"Shouldn't she get a free tiramisu or something since it's her bachelorette party?" one girl asked, pointing to the bride-to-be with a silver Tiffany's bracelet dangling from her wrist. In their world, everything was free.

Some Trixie/Chad couples eating at Paronelli's managed to get into a fight before they had a chance to order dessert. Occasionally a Trixie, with her mascara running, would leave the table in tears after hearing her Chad say the dreaded words, "I think we need some time apart." (Subtext: "Look, babe, having a girlfriend is ruining my old player image with the frat brothers. I need to resume my usual bar rotation with them and go back to being a male slut, but I can't do that with you always around.")

That's not to say there wasn't the occasional romantic success story as well. Katelyn was one of Haley's Trixie regulars who came in every few nights for a drink. Katelyn and her fiancé had their first date at Paronelli's, and he later proposed to her at the same table by the window where they sat on their first date. Her fiancé's name, ironically enough, was Chad.

Katelyn loved to talk about how romantic (and rich) Chad was. "He just bought me these earrings last week—they cost $3,000!" she gushed. "I always said I wanted my husband to treat me like a princess, and it looks like I'm going to get my wish." Katelyn was busy planning her wedding on the $150,000 budget her father had allotted for the event. She prattled on about Vera Wang and calla lilies. "Chad says that if I go over my budget, it's no big deal ... he'll chip in an extra $50,000 or more if it means I get what I want for my big day."

All the servers listened patiently to Katelyn's wedding details for as long as we could tolerate it, which was probably the reason we all got invited to the extravagant affair.

"I want everybody from the restaurant to be there," Katelyn said.

With an open bar, she'd probably get her wish.

The night of Katelyn's wedding, a couple of day servers got stuck working while the rest of us, including Hunter and Jordan in suit and tie, walked to the ceremony at a Catholic church in Old Town. The wedding was uneventful aside from the moment Chad's frat brothers donned sunglasses for the recessional.

After Katelyn's fifteen bridesmaids filed out of the church, a line of trolleys pulled up to escort the wedding party and the wedding guests through the city to the front door of the Westin hotel downtown. As we waited to board a trolley, Haley and I talked about how it was going to be funny to watch Hunter and Jordan sipping wine in their suits, forced to make small talk with other wedding guests while being transported to the reception. But, unwilling to rise to the occasion, Hunter and Jordan instead attracted the attention of the Chicago Police Department after chucking empty Miller Lite bottles from the back of the trolley into city garbage dumpsters as they drove past.

The wedding reception was as lavish as expected with hors d'oeuvres stations from twelve different countries, followed by a five-course meal. There were ice sculptures of castles and a two-story chocolate fountain cascading with every fruit known to man. There were five drink stations, one specifically monopolized by the Paronelli's crew. There was also an orchestra playing next to a rotating dance floor.

The reception experience was surreal, and, as Haley and I shared a cab back to Lincoln Park, she turned to me and said, "Katelyn is *so* lucky. I hope I marry a guy just like Chad someday and have a wedding twice as big as hers!"

Eleven months later, Katelyn and Chad divorced.

I arrived for my usual Monday night shift with Hunter and was surprised to see Haley filling in for him.

"Does Hunter have a show tonight?" I asked her.

"Oh, you didn't hear?" Haley said. "Hunter got fired. I guess he got drunk at Katelyn's wedding and told Mr. Paronelli what he really thought of him." I couldn't believe it.

Hunter's regulars were not at all happy about the recent turn of events. Several even left the restaurant to walk across the street and see if Hunter might be drowning his unemployment sorrows at The Bar.

Haley was in an unusually perky mood despite all the drama. She said she was so happy because she and Jackson had finally resolved their latest fight. Apparently Haley was supposed to have met Jackson at John Barleycorn's at one in the morning last weekend after she went to a concert at the House of Blues. By three, however, she still hadn't showed. At three fifteen, she sent Jackson a text message that said, "I'm sooo sorry. I can't make it. I've been hanging out with Bone Thugs-n-Harmony!"

Jackson wasn't angry that Haley had ditched him. He wasn't even angry that she was hanging out with other guys—famous other guys. He was only angry that she had used an exclamation point in her text message when describing her night's activities. He told her, "I *refuse* to associate myself with any girl who is *that* excited about hanging out with Bone Thugs-n-Harmony."

"How did you resolve the whole fight?" I asked Haley.

"Jackson called me after I got home the night of Katelyn's wedding," she said. "He told me he wanted to come over and that he missed me and thinks he might be in love with me."

"You let him come over?" I asked.

"Of course," she said. "He's never used the 'L' word before." The lame loser had finally said he loved her.

"So basically Bone Thugs-n-Harmony brought you and Jackson to a crossroads," I said, "and now you're back together?"

Haley smiled. "Yep, fo' shizzle."

In Hunter's absence, I was taking care of some of his regulars, including eighty-six-year-old Arturo.

"Arturo, do you want your usual cup of minestrone tonight?" I asked.

"Why aren't you married?" Arturo asked.

I hadn't been asked the marriage question in a while. In rural areas and cities in the Bible belt, people who were twenty-two and still single were sometimes treated like lepers. But in urban areas and cities like Chicago, people were considered abnormal if they were married under the age of thirty.

I told Arturo the truth—I was finding it hard, very hard, to meet quality men.

"You know why that is, right?" he asked. "Most of the quality men that *should* be living right now were never born."

The two words "never born" linked to the file in my brain that contained scenes from *It's a Wonderful Life*. I instantly saw George Bailey running through the center of Bedford Falls, shouting, "Merry Christmas!" I saw the Building and Loan, the original Bert and Ernie, Clarence the angel ... I stopped short of humming "Buffalo Gal (Won't You Come Out Tonight)."

"What do you mean they were never born?" I asked Arturo.

"What happened is that most of the good American men died in World War II, and then all the freaks that were left over multiplied."

I had recently read Stephen Ambrose's *D-Day* and *Band of Brothers*, and I thought Arturo might really be onto something.

"I didn't know you were a veteran, Arturo ..." I said.

"I'm not," he replied. "I'm one of the freaks who multiplied."

Hunter was fired by a drunk Mr. Paronelli at Katelyn's wedding at 1:17 a.m. He was rehired by a drunk Mr. Paronelli at The Bar at 3:31 a.m. the following Friday. "Three times the charm!" Hunter announced to the bar, fist in the air.

Saturday night we celebrated Hunter's return at The Bar. Even as people congratulated him, he mocked them, proving that the delicate social balance of all our lives had returned to normal. When Mark mentioned he had been working on fixing up a vintage car in his garage, Hunter shouted, "Mark, my friend, you *are* America!" When I complained to Jordan that my favorite sushi restaurant was now putting a slice of cucumber in each customer's water to add freshness and I didn't care for it, Hunter shouted, "Cucumbers are the new lemons! It's craaaazy, I tell you!"

Hunter started in on his questions about religion again, spouting off something about Christians being the last proponents for slavery. I noticed whenever religious debates started at The Bar, Haley remained silent, maybe not realizing that her beliefs were self-evident. Haley worshipped the trends of the marketplace. That was it. Unless someone was talking about a boutique where she could get a caramel-mocha-latte-colored purse to match her seventy-sixth pair of open-toed stilettos, she wasn't fully engaged in conversation.

In the *Journal of the American Academy of Religion*, David R. Loy said, "Our present economic system should also be understood as our religion, because it has come to fulfill a religious function for us ... Its god, the Market, has become a vicious circle of ever-increasing production and consumption by pretending to offer a secular salvation."

Haley, bored with Hunter's manifesto, stood next to me with an arm around my shoulders and bent over to say something in my ear. She was holding her fourth gin and tonic (a drink with an allure I never could grasp), and her words were slurred and slow. "I just wanted to say ... that you're my good friend ... 'cause Trish and Mel and Amy ... I mean, they're my Alpha sisters ... so they're, like, my *girls* ... but they're also, like, kinda slutty ... and they stab me in the back sometimes ..." She was making very little sense, but I could tell she wanted me to understand what she was saying. "I don't trust them ... so at least that's good ... I mean, it's not good that I don't trust them ... it's just good that I know I can't ... so that way I don't tell them stuff ... except sometimes I do when I'm wasted and forget ... then they throw everything in my face sometimes ... and call me a skinny you-know-what ... even though that's not what a real friend does ..." She squeezed my shoulders tighter. "So instead I just wait and tell everything to you ..." she said. "That's why ... you know ... Wednesday is my favorite day of the week."

I was touched.

SIX

ZEN AND THE ART OF WAITING TABLES

*"Like a beautiful flower, brightly colored and scented,
even so useful is the well-uttered speech of one who acts accordingly."*
—Buddha

Rachel's love life was starting to pick up. She went out on a date with a customer she met at the Gap. He was a former *Real World* cast member who shall remain nameless, and Rachel had a nice time with him. She hadn't seen his particular *Real World* season, but I had seen a few episodes, and I knew he was one of the biggest players ever to be on the show. I insisted that Rachel rent his season before going on a second date with him. She got so disgusted with his antics after watching just three shows that she never again answered his calls.

Following her first reality-TV mishap, Rachel met a guy at the grocery store who had been on *Fear Factor*. He had no issues to speak of (except for the fact that he had been dumb enough to go on *Fear Factor*). He was a well-adjusted, Catholic-born-and-raised personal trainer who seemed like a genuinely decent guy. He and

Rachel were hanging out about once a week.

"It's just so nice to be around someone who's totally normal in this city," Rachel said. "I love knowing that he won't start reading friendship poetry to me at any given moment."

I was happy for Rachel. Reality had finally delivered.

My own love life was another story entirely. Mark held the door open for me each time I walked into the restaurant—a little gesture that bothered me even though, after closer observation, I noticed that he held the door open for all the servers. My issue with him dealt with his proclaimed crush on me that loomed at the forefront of my mind. He told me he liked me, and I was honest and said flat-out, "I'm not interested in you. Sorry." It was a first for me. I was usually such a valiant protector of other people's self-esteem that I rarely employed brutal honesty. However, I wanted to turn over a new leaf now that I was out of college.

Mark looked pained for two days following the incident, but then, unexpectedly, he invited me to Dim Sum brunch in Chinatown one Sunday, "strictly as friends." I went, we had a nice time, and it seemed like he was 100 percent recovered and back to his old self. Even so, I couldn't help but continue to read romantic hopes into his every move.

Mark was a Zen Buddhist semi-pro wrestler with a dark purple beard (a contrast to his head of bleached blond hair). He had light blue eyes so clear that in certain lights I couldn't tell where his irises stopped and the whites of his eyes began. Even though he was just a couple of inches taller than I was, he walked with the inflated stride of a body builder. He wrestled under the alter ego

"Grim Reaper," and his dream was to become as well known as the WWE wrestler Triple H.

Mark was also on Prozac, but I was the only person privy to that information. I thought he might be on some kind of antidepressant the first day I met him because he smiled continually.

I liked Mark overall as a person, but I often felt a nagging annoyance when I was around him. Maybe it was because of his quiet voice and soft demeanor—a stark juxtaposition to his compact physique and Grim Reaper persona, or maybe it was because I was still bothered by what I described to Rachel as "the fire hydrant incident."

I was riding with Mark down a busy street when he suddenly jumped out of the car at a four-way stop, ran over to a city fire hydrant, turned it on, and stuck his head in the spurt of water. When I asked him to explain what had just occurred and why, he shook his head and let out a little growl under his breath. I didn't press the issue further.

On the other hand, I did appreciate Mark, not only for his patience while training me at Paronelli's, but also for sitting silently outside with me on warm nights, watching the raccoons scavenge through the restaurant dumpster. Not every twenty-seven-year-old American male would be patient enough for that activity.

Mark and I worked together on Thursday nights.

His current life crisis involved a $2,500 bill he received for Zulu's recent gastrointestinal surgery.

Zulu was Mark's cat. He was obsessed with her. This was an all-consuming, abnormal obsession. He would take the night off from work if he thought Zulu looked unhappy. He would spend hours lying in bed with Zulu, petting her while listening to Yanni.

"I just don't know how I'm going to get that money," Mark said.

"Work more shifts," I said.

"I can't," he said. "The Grim Reaper's following is really starting to grow. I need to ride out this wave."

I found several things wrong with Mark's response, the most obvious being his reference to himself in the third person. Secondly, I was disturbed by the fact that the Grim Reaper was gaining "a following." Finally, the surfing analogy didn't seem to fit the wrestling context.

The whole pro and semi-pro wrestling world fascinated me ... for only it could turn a cat-loving, Zen-sitting, Yanni-listening man into the ultimate master of death. I knew precious little about the WWE except that Rachel and I could only stomach about ten minutes of it at a time. When we stumbled across it while channel surfing, we marveled at how one wrestler with an insidious name would suddenly "call out" another menacing character—usually his greatest rival. And then, to the crowd's utter shock and amazement, the announcement would be made that that particular arch nemesis just happened to be in the building right that second—*and* he was ready and willing to fight.

"Did you wrestle last night?" I asked Mark as I filled up the salt and pepper shakers before the rush.

"Nope, I stayed home last night and ... just basically hung out." Mark couldn't hide his guilty look.

I groaned audibly. "Let me take a wild guess ... your night consisted of ... oh, smoking weed perhaps?"

"I cut back. I told you that."

"By how much?"

"I'm only smoking on the days I don't wrestle."

"You only wrestle twice a week. Are you supposed to be smoking reefer while you're on your meds?" I asked.

"Shhhhhh ... I swear you have the loudest indoor voice of anyone I have ever met," he said. "You want to get me fired, talking about my pharmaceutical habits like that for everyone to hear?" I wasn't sure which pharmaceutical habits he was trying to hide—the marijuana or the Prozac.

I courteously lowered my voice a few decibels. "Exactly *who* is going to fire you? Brad?" Mark smiled. "You smoked with Brad last night again?" I asked. "You really need to stop hanging out with him." I sounded like a mother scolding her son. I wouldn't have spoken that way to a guy I was romantically interested in; I knew mothering a man was terribly unattractive—which was the very reason I so freely scolded Mark.

"If I don't hang out with Brad, I'll just hang out with my high school buddies," Mark said. The implication was that no matter whom he hung out with, marijuana would be smoked.

"Or I could hang out with you more ... maybe go to your apartment sometime after work ... watch some TV—strictly as friends, of course," he said. The words "strictly as friends" seemed to be his new buzz phrase when he wanted to get his way. The last time Mark invited himself over to my apartment to hang out, he said, much to my chagrin, "We could watch a little tube," which made it easy to say no.

"I don't think Rachel would like me bringing some strange guy home," I said.

"Poor excuse," Mark said. "I'm hardly 'some strange guy.' I talk to Rachel every time she comes in here."

I tugged at Mark's purple beard. "This isn't strange?" I asked. I wondered why Mr. Paronelli didn't require Mark to wear a hairnet on his beard. I tried to imagine how disgusting it would be to find a purple beard hair intertwined in fettuccine.

"Do you have any idea how many lovely ladies would kill for just one date with the Grim Reaper?" Mark asked.

"No pun intended," I added.

"I already know that you're not interested in me like *that*," Mark said. "But it's too bad we can't even hang out as friends."

"Guilt trips don't work on me," I said. "And I *did* hang out with you just last week. We went to Dim Sum, remember? I thought we had a nice time too, so don't ruin it now."

It was actually en route to said brunch that the fire hydrant incident occurred, overshadowing the semi-pleasant conversation that had followed.

"Are you going to The Bar tonight?" Mark asked.

"Maybe," I said.

"Perfect," Mark said. "You and me ... Bar Next Door ... hangin' out tonight ... done."

I had a flashback to high school when my friend Lisa got asked to prom by a guy named Keith who drove past her house in a rusty brown Celica and shouted, "Hey, Lisa ... you and me ... Prom 1995 ... Let's *do* this thing!" Lisa just shook her head afterward, saying, "My life is a freaking joke," over and over.

Now *my* life was the freaking joke because the moment Mark began his whole "You and me ... hanging out tonight" spiel, Hunter walked into the restaurant and overheard it. He couldn't resist pausing to make fun of us. "So *that's* what you two are all about ..." He looked down his nose at me with incredulity. "You guys have a mad hot date tonight at The Bar! The Dalai Lama and the Jesus freak ... who would've guessed ..."

"Mark and I are not 'all about' anything," I assured Hunter.

"In her dreams we are," Mark countered like a fifth-grader as he walked away to tend to one of his regulars.

With Mark out of earshot, I further pled my case to Hunter. "Just so you know, there is absolutely *nothing* going on between Mark and me. We do *not* hang out alone outside of work, so don't start getting any ideas or spreading any rumors."

"Is that so?" Hunter said, his arrogant smile widening by the second. "Well, I think you missed your Liar's Club meeting tonight then ... because one of my friends saw you and Mark at Dim Sum last Sunday."

I was caught, fair and square. Before I could spout out any justification, Hunter said with mocking enthusiasm, "So you're all about the blond bombshell then? Tell me, is it a *total souplex* of the heart?" He began cackling.

I asked Hunter which of his friends had seen us together in Chinatown—not that it really mattered. I just wanted him to start talking so he would stop with the evil cackle.

"My fat friend Darcy saw you," he said.

"Not cool, Hunter," I said. "I've seen Darcy in here before, and she is *not* fat."

"Yeah right, she's not fat," Hunter said. "The only reason I'm even friends with her is so she won't eat me." He resumed cackling as I shook my head.

"It's true," Hunter said. "I have a different reason for each of my friendships. I only talk to *you* because your dad keeps dropping checks in the mailbox for me."

When we got to The Bar, I inhaled deeply. I loved the smell of smoke—to the extent that I purposefully didn't wash my clothes after I had been in a smoky place. One of my aunts smoked when I was young, and I must have psychologically associated the smell of smoke with getting to hang out with my cousins.

The Bar Next Door had a colossal fish tank along one wall. The first time I saw the hundreds of tropical fish swirling around inside, I let out an audible gasp. The rest of the décor, however, had been neglected—maybe to pay for the purchase and upkeep of such a nice fish tank. The floor was filthy, the bar stools broken, and the walls cracked and bare. Even the jukebox looked like it would collapse at any moment. The light from the fish tank made it possible for the bar to get away with using a few strategically placed candles for the remainder of its lighting, so it was clear that their money wasn't being spent on a high electric bill. No one complained about the disheveled appearance, though, because everyone was just satisfied to be in a bar where very few Trixies and Chads hung out. There were plenty of other Big Ten bars nearby, including an "Indiana bar," an "Iowa bar," and an "Ohio bar." But The Bar Next Door looked less like the Midwest and more like the Wild West, with three old men in cowboy hats sharing a pitcher of beer by the front windows.

I ordered my usual Cherry Coke and left Rachel a voice mail to stop by The Bar after she got off at the Gap. The moment I got off the phone, Mark asked, "Do you ever meditate?"

What was it about The Bar Next Door that promoted religious discussion before the liquid courage could even kick in?

"That was a random question," I said.

"I'm a random kind of guy."

"No, you're not."

It was obvious Mark had only asked me the question because he wanted me to ask him in return.

"I don't meditate. Do *you* meditate?" I said.

"I meditate every day for a half hour when I get up," Mark said.

"So you're into the Soto school of Zen?" I asked.

"How'd you know that?"

"I just know there are two schools of Zen practice," I said. "The Rinzai school of Zen focuses on sudden enlightenment through riddles or koans, and the Soto school of Zen encourages cross-legged meditation or zazen sitting."

Mark looked impressed. "I suppose you know how Zen itself started too," he said.

"Didn't Bodhidharma meditate for nine years straight?" I asked. "He even cut his eyelids off or something."

"That's the rumor," he said.

"And, yes, I know that Buddhism is to Hinduism what Protestantism is to Catholicism, if that's what you're about to ask me about ..." I said.

"I wasn't," he said. "But good work."

I knew it was stereotypically Western to become mesmerized by Eastern thought, but that still didn't stop me from studying a little Buddhism during college.

Mark said he believed meditation was vital for learning to live in the moment.

"What gave everyone the idea that living in the moment is the best way to live?" I asked. "Maybe we were only meant to live in our memories of the past and our hopes for the future."

I personally didn't want to "live in the moment." I was a twenty-two-year-old college graduate rehashing my limited Zen knowledge in a bar with a dude sporting a purple beard and hailing to the pseudonym Grim Reaper.

"After I meditate, I go through my day without expectations," Mark said. "Without expectations, I don't experience the pain of not having my expectations met."

When I thought of expectations, I thought of movies. If someone tells me, "It was the best movie I've ever seen! You have to see it!" the movie is automatically ruined for me. No matter how good it is, it never lives up to my expectations. On the other hand, if someone tells me, "That movie was a terrible waste of money," I can almost always find redemptive value in it, or at the very least I'll say, "It wasn't *that* bad."

How was it possible to extradite all expectations? When I take my first sip of my Mocha Blast, I expect it to taste sweet. When I go to a Second City show, I expect it to make me laugh. When I see customers pray before their meal, I expect them to leave me a small tip. In some ways, expectations make life bearable because things are more predictable and knowable. If Mark was truly able to give up his expectations, I wondered why he had been so bothered when he learned I wasn't romantically interested in him.

"So you feel no pain because you have no expectations?" I asked. "And you have no expectations because you spend time meditating each morning?"

"That's about right," Mark said.

I suspected he was giving meditation the praise that Prozac deserved.

Something happened to Siddhartha Gautama, the man who became Buddha, in his twenties that I could identify with. He became discontent with life. His newfound restlessness prompted him to venture away from his home to see if there was more to life than the luxuries his father had always lavished upon him. Along the roadside, Siddhartha saw a hunched-over, toothless man and was shocked because he had, until then, been sheltered from old age, illness, and death. His discovery of pain caused him to wonder if his own existence of pleasure was futile, so he did what many people facing such an epiphany continue to do—he went to the other extreme. He embraced asceticism, thinking total self-denial might be the best way to live. He ate as little as six grains of rice a day. But it wasn't long before he recognized that self-denial was getting him no further than self-indulgence. That was when he decided to sit beneath the now-infamous Bodhi tree, vowing not to move until he understood the reality of all things and the goal of existence. After sitting for seven days, he became enlightened and found "the middle way." He became the Buddha. The word "Buddha" simply means "a fully enlightened being," and Buddha taught that each individual has the capacity to become enlightened.

Buddha traveled across India for forty-five years teaching his newfound truths, or Dharma. I asked Mark to refresh me on Buddha's eightfold path. "There are eight 'Rights,'" Mark said.

"If you follow them, they will give you the best life possible. The Right View is about not holding on to any particular opinion, idea, concept, or belief. Our minds want to package everything into good and bad, but issues are more complex than that. Boxing up things in life makes us feel like we know something, but we only do it so we don't have to grapple with reality—which is a lot messier. Our mind must be a beginner's mind and can be compared to an empty rice bowl. If a bowl is already full, the universe can't fill it. But if it's empty, it has room to receive. Buddha taught that a person must empty his mind of all preconceived notions if he is to truly understand the Dharma. If a person learns any new idea while holding on to his old beliefs, he is not able to see the new teaching for what it really is. When we already have opinions and ideas, we aren't completely teachable."

"Isn't it virtually impossible to come to anything without a preconceived belief?" I asked.

"It's easier if you try to have Right Intention," Mark said. "That's the intention to be awake in this moment. It means that your mind can't be thinking past thoughts or about what else might be out there to learn."

"So that's why you guys are so big on living in the moment," I said. "Because if you live in the moment it's actually possible to have that beginner's mind you talked about."

"Yeah," Mark said. "If you're living in the moment, your speech and actions will flow from a real place and not from an image that you've believed yourself to be in the past. Right Speech is about making sure you are in tune with your authentic self, moment by moment, expressing whatever is in your heart. Right Speech is also refraining from any unnecessary, crude, undignified, or disturbing speech, including gossip and triviality. Right Action is any action that comes from a mind that carries no predetermined thought constructs."

Mark went on to explain that Right Livelihood is about earning a living through work that encourages insight, honesty, and harmony. Right Effort is learning to stop trying to control or improve a situation, others, or ourselves. Right Mindfulness is focusing on the constant chatter of dialogue in our minds in order to be released from it, and Right Meditation teaches us to refocus our minds on the here and now.

When I first heard Buddha's story, it sounded implausible that any person could be wholly removed from the pain of the world until his twenties. Then I took a closer look at my twentysomething peers and noticed they mainly associated with people in their own age group and social class. By doing this, most twentysomethings *had* managed to avoid the unpleasant parts of life thus far. They rarely visited hospitals, nursing homes, hospices, or homes for the mentally or physically disabled. Instead, they spent all their time in ultra suburban locales, like upscale malls and clubs, where it was easy to forget that 99 percent of the world is not young, healthy, and well off. They easily forget that matching accessories are not a priority for most women, and most men can't afford a $75 tie, let alone make use for it.

I told Mark that there were two Buddhist stories I really liked. The first explains the nature of enlightenment.

> A student asks a Zen master, "How long will it take for me to become enlightened if I really work hard at it?" The Zen master says, "Ten years." The student says, "No, I mean, if I really, really work at it ... how long will it take?" The Zen master says, "Twenty years."

The second story is about the nature of suffering in the human condition.

A Buddhist says the human condition is like a person who gets shot with an arrow. He is in a lot of pain because of his wound. But instead of getting help to alleviate his pain and suffering, he starts to ask questions like "Who shot that arrow at me?" and "What type of bow do you think he used?" and "Which city do you think the man who shot me came from?" and "Where do you think he ran off to?" He continues to ask all these questions, while overlooking his immediate problem—the pain and suffering he is experiencing from being shot with an arrow.

"I understood what Buddhists believe after I heard the story about the arrow," I told Mark. "Buddhists don't understand why humans spend all their time asking about the origin of the world and the end of the world, while forgetting about the pain and suffering of the present moment."

"Exactly," Mark said. "Buddha told people not to waste time on unanswerable questions, like whether the soul is one thing and the body is another or whether there is a heaven or hell. There just isn't time for those questions when we should all be busy doing good deeds to help alleviate the pain of those around us."

Although I understood what Mark was saying, I didn't fully agree—but I couldn't articulate why, and that bothered me. Mark looked past me to the door of The Bar. "Hey, look who it is," he said. Rachel had just walked in. Mark stood up and gave her a hug.

"Grim Reaper, what's up?" Rachel asked. She was a good sport to hang out with my coworkers, although odds were good that many of her own coworkers would show up at The Bar within an hour or two.

"We've just been talking about Buddhism," Mark said. "Your

roommate here knows more than I ..." Mark was cut off by Kyle, the bartender, shouting from behind the bar, "Hey, everybody, listen up! Brad's got a special number for us!" Brad, my manager at Paronelli's Pasta, jumped up onto a chair, while Hunter and Jordan, whom I hadn't even seen enter The Bar, began rhythmically chanting, "Brad! Brad! Brad!"

"What's all this about?" I asked Mark.

"When Brad's really out of it, he always asks Kyle if he can practice one of his opera songs," Mark said. "I guess he's been taking lessons."

Brad silenced the crowd and belted out an Italian ballad. He wasn't half bad. I tried to live in the moment, as strange as it all was. Rachel and I were sitting next to the Grim Reaper, who was swaying to the bellowing voice of our inebriated restaurant manager while the Sidewalks in Hell band members loudly cheered him on by the light of The Bar's tropical fish tank.

SEVEN

A NEW ANGLE

"Faithlessness is not lack of faith but faith in nothing."
—*A Course in Miracles*

Years ago, my friend Sebastian got into a heated fight with his ex-girlfriend Jill. They were arguing over the status of their relationship. Jill was yelling at Sebastian, and she told him that if he didn't make a commitment to her, she would break off the relationship. After she finished shouting all her frustrations at him, she asked, "So what are you thinking about right now?"

Sebastian replied, "Electrons."

To his credit, Sebastian's response was a culmination of weeks spent studying electrons in his organic chemistry class. While Jill was yelling at him, he was thinking about whether his and Jill's chemistry would ever mix well or if there would always be some kind of weird imbalance in their subatomic particles.

I wondered if my chemistry with Chicago would ever mix, or if the subatomic balance would forever be a little off.

Rachel and I were still less than thrilled about the direction our lives had taken. But the greatest benefit of working was that it filled up a lot of time we might have otherwise used to feel sorry for ourselves. Our old days of lamenting about our lives at Dunkin' Donuts had slowly evolved, and now our afternoons were filled with new stories.

Rachel was no longer dating the nice guy from *Fear Factor*. She said there was nothing wrong with him, which made the breakup all the more difficult. "Something was just missing," she said. I told her she couldn't hang onto a relationship just because there was nothing definably wrong. "You wouldn't want someone to do that to *you*, would you?" I asked. Rachel decided to move on.

"You remember the cute customer at the Gap I was telling you about?" she asked while sipping her Dunkaccino.

"His name was Solomon, right?" I asked.

"Yes ... and no," she said. "His name was Solomon until he came into the Gap the other day and told me he was having his name legally changed."

"Why?"

"Because he wants a name that means 'He Who Possesses the Heavens' in German."

"Is he German?"

"No."

"Wait," I said. "He wants a name that means 'He Who Possesses the Heavens'?"

"Yeah," Rachel said. "He says it's something about refusing to be restricted to just one astrological sign."

"And you *liked* this guy?" I said.

"Until I found all this out," she said.

"So what's his legal name now?" I asked.

"Er Der Die Himmel Besitzt."

"What?" I almost spit out a mouthful of Mocha Blast.

"He told me I can call him 'Er Der Die' for short," Rachel said.

"He seriously told you to call him that?" I couldn't get over it.

"What about that guy Rob you work with?" I asked. "Didn't you say he's really funny?"

"He is," Rachel said. "But another girl from work used to date him, and she says he's weird."

"Weird how?" I asked.

"I guess he told her he had 'walked with lions' in a previous life," Rachel said. "He even owns a bathrobe that says, 'King of the Kings of Beasts' on the back."

"Are you *sure* these people are for real?" I asked. Rachel and I had spent one, if not two, full days at Dunkin' Donuts pondering whether or not we might have accidentally stumbled upon an elaborate *Truman Show*-like ruse where we were the only real people and everyone else we met was merely an actor in an enormous show.

"Do you think I'm meeting all these crazy guys because I'm being punished for dumping such a nice, normal guy?" Rachel asked.

"Miss, I'm sorry to interrupt you ..." Norm, a Dunkin' Donuts employee, tapped me on the shoulder.

"There's a Brad on the phone for you."

I raised my eyebrow at Rachel, walked to the counter, and took the phone.

"Could you *please* come in an hour early tonight?" Brad asked. "We're getting busy."

"It's called a cell phone, Brad," I said.

"I know, but most servers don't answer when I call them from the Paronelli's phone."

He was right; I wouldn't have. But was a call to Dunkin' Donuts really necessary?

I got up to leave, still shaking my head over Rachel's story.

That was the first, but by no means the last, time Brad tracked me down at Dunkin' Donuts. Every few weeks, Norm would tap my shoulder, and without a word, I would walk to the counter and retrieve the phone. I once had Norm lie and tell Brad I hadn't come in that day, but within five minutes Brad walked from Paronelli's to Dunkin' Donuts and caught me in the midst of my deception.

"I need you to come in today." He sounded very irritated.

"She's busy," Rachel said. "Can't you see that?"

I was drinking my Mocha Blast with my feet up on the table.

"Rachel, I'm surprised you're so quick to get mouthy with me," Brad said. "You must have temporarily forgotten how good of friends I am with Carol."

Carol was Rachel's boss at the Gap. Rachel said no more.

"So are you coming into work?" Brad asked me. "Or do you want to get fired?"

I went into work. Only later did I learn that Brad's threats were as idle as my life, and that Mr. Paronelli was the only person who had ever actually fired anyone.

I had the displeasure of meeting the elusive and ever-intimidating Mr. Paronelli my first day on the job. He was a bald, middle-aged, divorced, unhappy jerk. Without so much as a "Hi, nice to meet you," he immediately turned to Brad and said, "Did you make sure she read the policies and procedures manual? Does she know that I'm not afraid to fire her if she [screws] up?" Then, rather than continue to talk about me in front of me, he finally turned to me and said, "Listen, babe, waiting tables at my restaurant is a job a lot of people would love to have. So don't [mess] it up. But if you do, you can guarantee I'll put up the Help Wanted sign in the window and have twenty kids lined up outside in minutes begging me for your job. Always remember how dispensable you are." He had really rolled out the red carpet.

Fortunately Mr. Paronelli himself wasn't around much. He left all the day-to-day managerial duties to Brad. Brad was also middle-aged and divorced, but he had a full head of brownish-red hair and a distinctive red mustache that could almost be classified as a handlebar, although Brad himself would likely contest such a label. He was lazy—lazy with his facial hair and lazy with his management style.

Brad was a passive-aggressive whom no one took seriously. He was more passive than aggressive, generally uncaring about what the servers did or how they did it. I soon learned that his relaxed demeanor might be partially and/or wholly attributed to the fact that most days he came to work stoned. His aggressive side was rare, but when it reared up, it always included the threat, "Do you want to get fired?" Brad became most aggressive when a server spoke disrespectfully to him. He didn't like anyone shattering the grand illusion that he was a legitimate, hard-working manager, worthy of respect and obedience. But one look into his glassy eyes, and few could take him seriously. Jordan held the record for "most termination threats" in one shift. He had garnered twelve, plus a bonus thirteenth threat of "Do you want me to boycott all your Sidewalks in Hell shows from now on?"

Brad worked Monday through Friday, but he hung out at Paronelli's all weekend—I supposed to be near *his* urban family. The fact that he never left the restaurant meant that even when he wasn't working, he had sufficient opportunity to threaten our illustrious serving careers from his perch at the bar.

Kyle from The Bar Next Door bet Brad $100 that Brad spent more "off the clock" time at work than he did. Brad insisted that although he might be older, his vision was still good enough to spot Kyle hanging out at The Bar on all his nights off. The bet had been in effect for two years, with no winner. That was because the bet's perimeters were absurd. In order to win, either Kyle or Brad had to *physically capture* the other person in his own place of employment on his day off. Twice, I had watched Kyle burst into Paronelli's, narrowly missing a fleeing Brad who escaped to the office and securely locked the door.

Brad's life hadn't been easy. He had been a few months away from becoming an ordained priest when he fell in love and scrapped his plans in order to get married. Two years into marriage, he learned his wife was cheating on him with his best friend. He gave up on her and Catholicism and talked Chris Paronelli, his old college buddy, into letting him manage Paronelli's Pasta.

Brad's current interest was opera, and he was taking voice lessons. Although his opera performances had been confined to The Bar, he had high aspirations for greater fame someday. I guess you could say he was an almost-priest turned operatic pothead.

After turning his back on Catholicism, Brad's spiritual interests shifted to New Age thought. When pressed hard enough, he could boil his entire worldview down to a purported claim that he once floated around his house at a forty-five-degree angle.

The first time Rachel stopped by the restaurant to visit me on her break, Brad viewed her as new ears for his old story. He explained the floating phenomenon in detail as she listened attentively. "When I started to float, I suddenly understood the purpose of existence," he said. "When I reached the forty-five-degree angle, I actually understood the levels of heaven and the breadth of the cosmos. It was only *at* the forty-five-degree angle that I received enlightenment." He would then launch into a narrative, complete with diagrams, about the different levels of heaven and how each one related to an inner light cloaked within our own consciousness. It felt like we were taking New Age Babble 101.

Rachel and I read a few books about ley lines early in college, and suddenly all things New Age had intrigued us. In fact, upon instruction of our yoga teacher or "sensei," as he had asked to be addressed, we started sleeping with our heads facing north to "balance out our charkas" or some other such nonsense. We also started granting validity to phrases like "I don't know, there's just something about his energy I don't like." We even went as far as researching a post-college move to Sedona, Arizona, the place where all energy points in the world converge. However, even for two girls who had been stupid enough to do all of the above, we still found Brad's metaphysical accounts to be a little far out.

Rachel and I would walk past Brad, tilting our bodies back, pretending to float, and saying, "Brad, check it out ... we're enlightened." He didn't find it funny.

Sometimes I wondered what else Brad smoked, but I didn't ask.

However, one day in front of Rachel (just for laughs) I asked, "Brad, why forty-five? Why not sixty-five? Or how about twenty-eight? A twenty-eight-degree angle would have been so much cooler!"

Brad got a defensive look in his eye. "I have told you girls before, but I'll tell you one more time," he said. "It was not until I reached the *forty-five*-degree angle that I understood."

"Understood what?" I asked.

"The universe, you dumb---!" he said.

I marveled that Brad was once nearly a man of the cloth.

But he was, and it was evidenced by the fact that he could readily quote long portions of Scripture. He told me and Rachel that he wanted to have the mind of Christ. I was confused as to how that fit in with his whole metaphysical angle (so to speak).

I had come to expect spiritual conversations each night at The Bar. Hunter and Brad were already discussing the meaning of life over Jack and Cokes when I decided to join in.

"Brad, what did you mean when you said you wanted to have the mind of Christ?" I asked.

"I believe the word 'Christ' is a psychological term that refers to the common thread of divine love, which is the essence of every human mind," Brad said. "The 'mind of Christ' is a mind that contains nothing but love."

Hunter shot me a look he only used when a member of The Goof Troop entered the restaurant.

Brad continued, "Jesus and others were enlightened beings because their perspective in life was consistently one of love even though they lived in a world of fear. If a person starts thinking with fear rather than love, he is in hell."

"So you would say that a lack of love is the source of all the world's problems?" I asked.

"Yes," Brad said. "Because whenever we perceive anything other than love, we are sinning. The only way to have our sins forgiven is to open up to love again. If we call on the Holy Spirit to help transform our thoughts from fear into love, the Spirit can deliver us from hell."

"Give me a more practical example," I said.

"Anytime you judge another person in any way, you're wrong even if you're right," Brad said. "God doesn't need us to police the universe. Shaking a finger at someone doesn't help him change. Our perception of someone's guilt only keeps him stuck in it. When a person behaves badly, it only means his behavior was derived from fear. It's our job to see through the illusion of guilt to the innocence beyond. God never condemned us, and a son of God cannot sin."

"Excellent!" Hunter said. He had been ignoring us and talking to Kyle, but suddenly he rejoined our conversation. "So you're saying I'm a son of God," he said loudly, with crazed eyes. "And you're saying since I'm a son of God, I can't sin ... hmm ..." Hunter let out a short, evil cackle and then turned around to continue talking to Kyle.

"How'd you go from Catholicism to all the beliefs you have now?" I asked.

"After my wife left me, I got bitter," he said. "I mean *really* bitter. Then I came across some teachings that explained how the ego always emphasizes what a person does wrong, but the Holy Spirit emphasizes what they do right. People's fearful patterns and dysfunctional habits cover up their true perfection. Once I understood that, I was able to start down the path of forgiveness because I saw that my ex-wife had been acting in fear and not love."

"And you forgave her?" I asked.

"Eventually," he said. "I didn't want to be dragged down into her negative energy, so I really had no choice but to forgive. Whenever a person falls prey to the negative energy around him or her, that person starts to lead others away from God. That is what happened to my wife because she had surrounded herself with messages coming from people who lived in fear and not love. I didn't want to get sucked into her world of fear, so I decided to harness the positive energy from people around me who had surrendered to love—that way I could create a life that would better others rather than harm them. The energy we allow ourselves to be susceptible to determines everything that happens in our lives. If we take in too much negative energy, we'll become physically sick. If we take in positive energy, we can heal ourselves. Every atom on earth resonates with either positive or negative energy. Even musical chords and colors can affect us positively or negatively, depending on what type of energy they are giving off. The source of all positive energy is God, and He's always there—just waiting for us to turn to Him."

I remembered reading the book *Embraced by the Light*. The author, Betty Eadie, believes we are all spiritual beings who were *with* God when He created the world. We later chose to come to earth to learn valuable lessons we could not learn in heaven. When we came to the planet, we agreed to be born with a "veil of forgetfulness" that would erase all our past memories of heaven.

Before we came to the earth, we chose our mission in life, and we covenanted with specific souls we were close to in heaven, promising to reunite with them on earth so they could help us complete our mission. We were able to choose the family we wanted to be born into and the time in history we would arrive on earth. We chose specific experiences that would contribute to our spiritual development before we came to the planet, including painful ones like divorce or job loss. Some people decided to come to earth poor to learn different lessons, and some chose to come to earth mentally handicapped to experience a different type of spiritual growth. Some chose to be alcoholics to induce compassion in those around them and teach their friends and family valuable lessons about love.

Because we all learn different lessons on earth, each of us has a different level of spiritual understanding at any point of time. Therefore, all the world's religions are necessary because there are people on earth who need the teachings of each one. Every religion can be used as a stepping stone to further our own spiritual growth, and, in the end, we all end up back in heaven ... wiser and happier.

Betty's take on existence was one of the most neat and tidy explanations I had ever heard.

Using her logic, I figured our courts might be a lot emptier if we could all agree that criminals had chosen specific crimes to commit beforehand, while they were still in heaven. Therefore these crimes, like everything else that happened on the planet, would only serve to accelerate their spiritual development. No need for a trial.

"You want to know something that took me way too long to figure out?" Brad asked. "This whole organized religion thing ..." he said, shaking his head disapprovingly. "Catholics and Protestants ... Episcopalians, Presbyterians, Lutherans, Methodists ... Evangelicals ... Baptists, Pentecostals ... it's all way too complicated, and it's all total B.S."

"Why do you say that?" I asked.

"Everyone's experience is different," he said. "It took me a while, but I finally realized my spiritual journey is my own, which means that I can't let other people tell me what my journey should look like. That's why I haven't been inside a church for years."

I had read that well-educated, middle-class people were beginning to leave churches and reject organized religion at an alarming rate. Most people were leaving to seek "personal enlightenment" in whatever form they could find it. They would embrace an individual religious psychology without the supportive attachments of a community of like-minded people. However, personal development on one's own is not only more difficult, but occasionally more dangerous than growing within a group. Connecting to other people is one of the best ways to prevent the isolation in life that can lead to depression. It is also one of the best ways to accelerate maturity—by learning to care about others and not live selfishly. Relationships are vital for good health.

I met a girl in college who told me she broke up with her fiancé and stopped hanging out with her girlfriends because she felt that God had "called" her to rely solely on Him to meet her needs. I guessed that this girl probably hadn't been "called" by the God of the Bible, because that God never once said to try to live life without other people. Common sense tells us that if a relationship is unhealthy, it shouldn't continue. But God never said people should drop *healthy* relationships with other people in order to better serve Him. There's neither truth nor logic in that.

"Each man must find his own way," Brad said. "And, fortunately for us, there is no *one* right way."

"There could be one right way," I said. "You can't know that there isn't unless you possess all the knowledge in the universe."

"I *did* possess all the knowledge in the universe for a few moments," Brad said.

"Oh yeah, I forgot," I said as I leaned forward in my seat, using the bar as support until I reached a forty-five-degree angle.

Hunter swiveled back around on his barstool. He pretended to check his watch, and in an absurdly loud voice, he asked, "Is it time to get enlightened?"

"Laugh all you want," Brad said. "But if you had floated, you would know."

Brad's admonition sounded like the perfect title, should he ever write a book.

EIGHT

COOK COUNTY

"He who knows contentment is rich."
—*Tao Te Ching*

Each day as Rachel and I entered Dunkin' Donuts and waved to our comrades, I thought about how deceptive Dave Matthews had been. He sings, "Turns out not where but who you're with that really matters." Yet where you are determines who you're with. Where you are is everything, literally. People don't give enough credit to the power a place holds, save environmental psychologists and feng shui consultants. But I was learning that my environment determined who I met, what I thought about, and especially how I felt.

Rachel was learning the same lesson. As we sat down at our Dunkin' Donuts table, she let out a long, frustrated sigh.

"Didn't go too well?" I asked, regarding her date the previous night.

She had gone out with Landon, a customer she met at the Gap. When Landon showed up at The Bar one night, I commented to Rachel that he had the most medieval-looking haircut I'd ever seen. Rachel laughed hysterically. I later learned she had thought I called his haircut "mid-evil," which made zero sense and definitely didn't deserve a laugh. Regardless, Landon asked Rachel out that night, and they began seeing each other regularly.

I liked Landon, even though I once heard him refer to a Nobel Prize winner as a Noble Prize winner, as in Barnes & Noble. Issues of pronunciation seemed to plague the relationship from the onset. I also thought Landon was a little premature when he told Rachel he wanted to celebrate their *one-month* anniversary from the day they met.

Landon's curious exuberance over a new relationship wasn't the first I'd seen of its kind. Meg, my freshman roommate in college, and a guy named Brice Potter celebrated their one-week anniversary from the first day they "made it official." One of Brice's friends had a video of him on day four of their "relationship" announcing to the camera, "I'm whipped."

Also, on spring break in Panama City, my friend Ann and a guy named Josh (whose last name she never learned) celebrated their twenty-four-hour anniversary with a romantic dinner. They had met in a mega-club on the beach after Ann approached Josh because she was curious why he was wearing a Burger King crown and doing jumping jacks in the middle of the dance floor. "Time stopped," she said. "'Country Grammar' was playing at the moment our eyes locked." The next morning they explained to their dumbfounded friends, "We were destined to meet. It was love at first sight. We're going out tonight to celebrate our twenty-four-hour anniversary." A few weeks and a few emails later, the short-lived romance faded along with Ann's tan.

Rachel, who is more gracious than me, didn't bat an eyelash when Landon asked to take her out for their anniversary.

"He had the night all planned out," Rachel said as we stood in line at Dunkin' Donuts. "First we went on a carriage ride downtown ... you know, the ones that start out at the old water tower ... then we had dinner at Carmine's."

"Not bad for one month," I said. "One year should be really good."

"I highly doubt there will be a one year," Rachel said.

"Why not?" I asked.

"Well, right after we got our appetizers at dinner, Landon stared at me and said, 'Sometimes you just *know*.'"

I burst into laughter. "Join the club," I said.

I too had fallen victim to the "sometimes you just know" expression as a senior in college. A skinny punk freshman named Donnie had stalked me all year, claiming I was the most beautiful woman he'd ever seen. (He also claimed to "feel naked" when he's wasn't wearing two pieces of ice in his left ear.) I told Donnie nothing would ever happen between us, but he still sent me a dozen roses and a handwritten note that said, "Sometimes you just know."

"Are you seriously going to break it off with Landon over that?" I asked.

"Most likely," she said. "Did you know Landon's from Nixa, Missouri?"

"Really?" I said. "Did you know Jason Bourne is from Nixa, Missouri?"

"Jason who?" Rachel asked.

"Jason Bourne ... *The Bourne Identity* ... *Supremacy*," I said. "Never mind."

"You just violated your own rule about actors and their screen names," Rachel said. "You should have said Matt Damon."

"Not true," I said, "because I was talking about the city that a character in the movie was from ... just forget it."

"Anyway, the whole reason I even mentioned Nixa is because that's where Lora is from," Rachel said. Lora was my other best friend in college, and we skipped class at least once a week to indulge in egg drop soup, the noon special at a Chinese restaurant near campus. Lora was with me the afternoon I received the roses and the note from Donnie.

"That's a little synchronistic, don't you think?" Rachel asked. "The first time you hear the cheesy line, you're *with* someone from Nixa, Missouri ... the first time I hear the line, it's coming *from* someone from Nixa, Missouri."

I rolled my eyes.

"I can't believe I almost forgot to tell you," Rachel said. "I think I saw Dr. Porter the other night when I was walking to Paronelli's to visit you on my break. This guy across the street looked *just* like Dr. Porter—trench coat and all. He was standing on the corner, yelling something at the passing traffic."

"That sounds about right," I said.

Provided Dr. Porter hadn't been a figment of our imaginations, I felt confident he would be out there somewhere, shouting to anyone who would listen: "Do something, anything!" And even though my life looked nothing like I had planned it to, I was still glad I had responded to Dr. Porter's call. His pretend Possibility Place had led me to a real place where I could be around real people ... and slowly resume a life among the living.

Goof Troop charter member Tarrah, chai in hand for me, entered Paronelli's after a prolonged absence. I thanked her for the drink and asked why we hadn't seen her in the past few weeks. She said she had just returned from a two-week trip to Washington, D.C. "It has to do with my project."

"Tarrah," Hunter interrupted, "tell us what your project is right this second, or I swear I'm telling all the wait staff to stop serving you." Tarrah laughed.

"I won't listen to him," I said. "I'll serve you no matter what."

"I feel bad, you guys," Tarrah said. "But I honestly can't tell you about what I'm working on. The only thing I really *can* tell you is that I was meeting with the head of the CIA to see if they might be interested in my project when it's all finished."

We had finally made some progress. With this new information, I believed her story more than ever.

"So let me get this straight," Hunter said. "You're telling me that you've been MIA due to the CIA?"

Tarrah was good-natured enough to give him a second laugh.

"It's the truth," she said. "I don't know what else I could possibly say to prove it to you."

Tarrah's words carried weight. Hunter was the ultimate skeptic, which wasn't necessarily a bad thing. The only problem was that occasionally, no matter how hard a person doubted or mocked or disbelieved something, it didn't change the fact that it was true. In those instances, the skeptic was the fool all along.

I wanted to tell Hunter about a book I had read called *The Myth of Certainty*. Author Daniel Taylor said,

> Cynicism may seem an intelligent position, given the hypocrisy and stupidity of many human endeavors. Cynics often pride themselves on their greater insight into human nature and society, fancying that they see through sham and pretensions that fool everyone else. Ultimately, however, cynicism is both foolish and cowardly itself. It is foolish because it underestimates the God-given human potential for finding and creating meaning in life, and it is cowardly because it is afraid to risk anything in the human adventure. The cynical spirit insists on certainty before it will affirm and, lacking that, retreats into the false security of denial.

"Clock in, guys!" Brad shouted.

I ignored him and asked Mario, one of the cooks, to make me some lobster-filled ravioli before my shift. Mario pulled his shiny black hair into a rubber band and put on his hairnet.

"You wants ongos y cebollas también?" Mario asked. I nodded yes to the mushrooms and onions. My continual conversation with the cooks consisted of their broken English and my broken Spanish.

"Gracias, mi amigo," I said.

Brad snuck up behind me and clamped a hand on my shoulder. "Tell me you didn't just order yourself some ravioli."

"I didn't just order myself some ravioli." I tried not to laugh.

"So basically, by lying to me, I can assume you're planning to get fired tonight?" Brad asked. I ignored him and poured myself an iced tea to drink with dinner. I knew my work ethic wasn't the greatest, but I didn't have the strength to take my job seriously.

The four Paronelli's cooks each worked ninety-six hours a week. They worked sixteen hours a day, six days a week.

The cooks' names were Mario, Juan, Juan, and Juan. They had come to the States to find jobs that would better support their families back in Mexico. While immigration debates raged around them, they concentrated on trying to make enough money to fly their wives and children to Chicago to live with them.

Anytime I needed help during my shift, I asked Mario or one of the Juans. They could answer any question I had and always had my back. "Watch out for Diablo Pelón," Mario warned. The cooks affectionately referred to Mr. Paronelli as Diablo Pelón—Bald Devil. It was fortunate that Mr. Paronelli didn't speak a syllable of Spanish. If the Bald Devil heard about a mistake made during a shift, he asked the cooks whose fault it was—theirs or the servers.

The cooks always took the blame, even though they rarely deserved it. Mario said they took the heat because they didn't want any of us to get fired. "Son familia," he said. We were like family.

Mario's most defining feature was his long black hair that was regrettably cut into a mullet but, thankfully, balanced out with a well-groomed goatee. Mario had a way of acknowledging people with a cocky nod that made me wonder if he had started a couple bar-room brawls accidentally by using it too carelessly. From the thick gold chain around his neck hung a cursive gold "Mario."

Sometimes to make me laugh, Mario would sarcastically string together the most obnoxious exit lines and deliver them in one long sentence to a customer leaving the restaurant: "Thank you very much ... Please come again ... We loved having you ... Don't forget we're open from eleven to eleven, seven days a week ... Tell your friends about us ... Have a great night ... Stay out of trouble ... We'll see you again soon ... Vote Mario Gonzales for President."

To keep the three Juans straight, we called them by their nicknames. The first Juan was "Uno" because he was the first Juan to ever work at Paronelli's. The second Juan was a bigger guy, and the cooks referred to him as Juan Grande, but we called him Primo or Cousin—both because he was Mario's cousin and because we didn't exactly feel comfortable calling him "Fat Juan." The last Juan we called Abuelo or Grandpa because he had at least thirty years on the other two Juans.

I spun around on a barstool as I watched Mario put butter and oil into a pan to cook my ravioli.

"Qué pasa, amigo?" I asked him.

"Nada, nada," he said.

"Uno, Primo, Abuelo ... qué pasa?" I shouted down the cook's line to the three Juans.

"Nada," all three Juans replied in unison. Their jinx was a freak accident, not a daily occurrence.

Nothing was going on for the cooks yet again today. Just the same daily flow of regulars in and out. Just the same plates of linguine and penne being served up over and over with assorted sauces ad infinitum.

"Tú bien, amiga?" Mario asked. I had already heard him ask Mark how he was doing, and his genuine concern for everyone around him impressed me.

"Amiga, check the schedule," Primo said. "I think it maybe change." Primo always kept a watch on the server schedule for me. Sometimes Brad got shifty with our shifts and didn't tell us. If there was any change made to my work hours, Primo let me know so I didn't get in trouble.

The cooks were all about making my life (and everyone else's lives) easier.

The more I got to know the cooks, the more I respected them. They only made $8.25 an hour because there weren't exactly overtime regulations for illegal immigrants. Like many other workers from Mexico, the guys kept precious little from their earnings, sending most of it back to their families.

The most extraordinary thing about the four men was that they were consistently happy. They never appeared tired, stressed, or preoccupied. They never got frustrated during a rush. They never tried to cut corners so they could leave work early. They never got too busy to help out a server in need. They were content to have the opportunity to work hard and try to make a better life for their families.

Whenever I panicked at the height of our dinner traffic, the cooks calmed me down by saying, "Tranquila, preciosa ..." If I forgot to punch in an order, the cooks threw the pasta dish together for me with lightening speed. They wanted to ensure my tables never had any reason to get hostile with me. "Blame it on us if the food is late," they would say.

I was making decent tips waiting on Lincoln Park's trust-fund Trixies; the cooks were making next to nothing standing along the steamy prep line for sixteen hours straight. If they could be tranquilo, I could too.

Every night after we clicked the Open sign to Closed, Mario went to the office to turn the Muzak system to a Spanish channel. He and Primo would then jump up onto the bar and salsa dance. It was a beautiful scene—cocky, tough guy Mario, reveling in life's simple pleasures before he had to clean the greasy stove, take out the trash, and lock up around midnight, only to return to the restaurant by seven the next morning.

One of my favorite nights since I moved to Chicago was when we threw a party at The Bar for Abuelo. We were rejoicing in his announcement that he was within weeks of earning enough money to fly his entire family over from Mexico. His wife, two daughters, and a son-in-law would soon be joining him. Abuelo was the first of the four cooks to reach the ultimate goal, proving to the others that their long hours of work weren't in vain. That night, for the first time in a long time, I remember feeling happy.

It was Thursday night, and rent was due Friday. Business had been slow, and for that reason I was still a full $250 short on my portion of the rent. I finished my lobster ravioli and breathed a silent prayer that I would somehow rack up $250 in tips in the next five hours. If I wasn't able to do it, we would probably have to ask Dan for yet another rent extension. Although I was sure Dan would be as gracious as he had been the first time we were late paying rent, I hated taking advantage of his kindness a second time.

Dan Jovanevic was one of the nicest men I had ever known. He had a thick Yugoslavian accent, and his eyes literally sparkled when he smiled. He had deep laugh lines around his mouth, and he spoke using sweeping hand motions that drew additional attention to his tall frame.

After we signed our lease, Dan took us with him to pick out new paint colors for our apartment. He also let us pick out new appliances, carpet, and linoleum. He said, "Don't look at the price because I don't care about money. I just want my tenants to be happy." After we picked out everything for our apartment, Dan took us to dinner with some of his Yugoslavian friends to celebrate. He dropped $600 on dinner and promised that anytime we needed another night out of the apartment, he'd gladly do it again.

Dan was nearing fifty and had no children. His wife had died of cancer years ago. He said he liked to spoil his tenants because he had no family to spoil. The same royal treatment we received was given to every tenant in our building. Dan had no hidden agenda; he just wanted people to like the place they came home to every night. He said he "felt so blessed to be alive" that he wanted to "share his joy and wealth with everyone."

Dan wasn't crazy or lonely; he was an authentically kind person. He was not discriminatory in his kindness either. He lavished everyone he met with compliments, praise, and encouragement. He made every individual feel loved and respected, whether young or old, rich or poor. It wasn't unusual for him to take a homeless man to lunch or to stop and tell an elderly woman that she was more beautiful now than she could have ever been when she was young. "True beauty comes with age," he would say.

Dan told us, "Even if you girls burn my whole building down, I would still have nothing but love for you in my heart!" The first time we asked Dan for a rent extension, he said, "Girls, you take all the time you need. Just pay it whenever you can. It's only money." Dan may not have been the savviest businessman on earth, but he was a superb human being.

One Saturday at two in the morning, Rachel tried calling her friend Dawn but accidentally dialed Dan instead. Dan groggily answered the phone, and Rachel apologized profusely for the mistake. Before she hung up, Dan asked, "Be honest ... is there anything at all in the apartment that you'd like fixed ... or anything at all that you want me to change?" Rachel said maybe he could stop by sometime next week to replace a busted window screen. Dan agreed to it.

A half-hour later—at half past two—Dan showed up at our place with a sleepy grin, carrying a new window screen under one arm. He installed it then and there.

He said, "I couldn't sleep because I kept thinking about how terrible I'd feel if something bad happened to you girls because of that broken screen. This just couldn't wait."

Dan had never darkened the door of a church, which was kind of funny to me because the last time I had visited a church, I heard a sermon about how Christians are supposed to be different—warm, caring, giving, helpful, compassionate, concerned with other people's welfare. The pastor said, "If you're a Christian, people will stop to ask you, 'Why are you so happy all the time?' or 'Why are you so nice to everyone?' or 'You always seem at peace ... what's your secret?'"

But that hardly ever happened to a single professed "Christian" I had met. However, it happened to Dan all the time.

When I performed a preliminary tip count after the dinner rush, I learned my total tips amounted to a mere $124.50, which meant I needed to make another $125 in the next two hours. The problem was that the restaurant was empty.

"Isn't Blues Fest tonight?" I asked Mario. "Everybody must be downtown, because obviously nobody's around here."

"It looks like somebody's around here," Mario said, nodding his head toward the door.

I turned to see a party of six walk in. There were three tall men, and each had a date on his arm.

As the men spoke, I immediately recognized a Yugoslavian accent among them. "Everyone, let me introduce you to one of my favorite tenants," Dan said as he hugged me and then made introductions.

Dan sat down at the bar and called out to Mario, "You guys are all taking good care of my tenant, right?"

Mario gave a hint of a nod and put up the collar of his shirt—apparently this was a new gesture he was trying out to indicate the affirmative.

Dan's positive attitude was infectious, and before long, I had forgotten my financial worries. Dan's "friend" Sheri was obviously interested in him. Even though Sheri was quiet, she watched Dan with soft eyes of admiration, and I hoped Dan would find love again.

When Dan and his friends left just before eleven o'clock, I was pleased at how quickly the time had passed. Then I caught sight of the dirty plates littering the bar and grimaced. Mario, always helpful, started cleaning up for me. The clanging sound of stacking dishes was halted temporarily when Mario said, "Amiga, there's something down here that belongs to you."

On the bar, next to a dirty plate of pasta, was a $150 tip. A napkin tucked beneath the money said, "I'm proud of your hard work and I'm here for you if you ever need anything. —Dan"

I laid my tips out on the bar to count.

"You made mucha moneda tonight," Primo commented on my stack of bills as he passed behind me with a stack of dirty dishes. Abuelo followed behind him carrying another bus tub piled high with glasses. "Muy bien, amiga," he said. "You made good tips."

They were praising me on a job well done and rejoicing in my good fortune, even as they cleaned up the filthy mess my customers had made.

Dan's commendation of my work ethic had already made me feel guilty for my usual laissez-faire attitude toward my job, and as I observed the work ethic of the cheerful cooks, my conscience grew guiltier still.

"I don't know how they do it," I mused to Brad.

"Do what?" he asked.

"They never complain," I said. "And they're always happy for me whenever I make a lot of money."

"Know what's crazy?" Brad asked. "I'm fluent in Spanish, and in all the years I've worked here, I've never once heard a single complaint out of any of them."

Now *that* was remarkable.

I waved goodbye to Brad and the cooks, trying to sneak out the front door before Mark saw me.

"Not a chance," Mark called out from the door of the wine cellar. "If you even think I'm letting you walk home alone tonight after those muggings last weekend, you're nuts."

I reluctantly agreed to let him walk me home. "You are *not* coming in to watch TV when we get to my place though," I said.

"That's not why I'm walking you home," Mark said, shaking his head. "I just want to make sure you're safe."

I had never been scared to walk alone in the city at any time of night, but I felt an additional level of comfort with Mark's presence. Certainly no one would tangle with me as I walked next to the Grim Reaper himself. Our conversation threaded through the usual topics: Zulu's recovery from surgery, Mark's recent wrestling match, meditation. But for the first time in a long while, nothing about Mark annoyed me. Or maybe it was simply that Dan had reminded me that even far away from home, I had people who would go out of their way to look out for me.

It was nice to walk home from work in the warm glow of the street lamps. With people out and about everywhere, the city streets had a much safer feeling than the empty roads of suburbia could ever hope to possess. Chicago suddenly didn't feel as cold or uncaring as I had previously judged it to be.

On the walk home, I resolved to improve my attitude about work. The cooks were teaching me that my job was a blessing, not a curse. I hoped their continual spirit of gratefulness would rub off on me. I also resolved to be a little kinder to Mark in the meantime. Dan had inspired me.

NINE

THE BUSINESS OF BELONGING

"Do not underestimate evil, thinking 'It will not approach me.' A water pot becomes full by the constant falling of drops of water. Similarly, the spiritually immature person little by little fills himself with evil."
—Buddha

"How was dinner with Jet Li last night?" I asked Rachel as we sat down at our usual table. Rachel's latest love interest was the brother of a fellow Gap employee. All Rachel had told me about him was that his name was Wes Kahn and that he resembled a young Jet Li.

"Overall, the date was good," she said. "There was just one minor incident."

"Tell me he didn't say 'sometimes you just know.'"

"He didn't," Rachel said. "But remember how I told you that the last time I saw Wes, he kept talking to me about some DJ friend of his named Mini Con."

"Yeah," I said, unsure as to how this was pertinent.

"So," Rachel continued, "last night after dinner, Wes and I are standing at the Belmont stop waiting for the L, and Wes asks me if I want to see Mini Con. I said sure, I'd like to go hear him, but first

I wanted to know what he did time for ... you know, I'm assuming he's an ex-con because of his DJ name."

"And ..."

"Wes tells me that the guy stole a chest from someone." Rachel started to laugh so hard she could barely choke out the rest of the explanation. "But I still agree to meet him."

"Is Mini Con a midget?" I interrupted.

"Not exactly," Rachel said, trying to catch her breath. "So we're still standing at the L stop when Wes suddenly yanks off his shirt ... and on his left pec is a huge tattoo of a cartoon character with Wes' face, standing in front of two turntables. And Wes says to me, 'Rachel, meet Mini Kahn'—as in the Miniature Wes Kahn. Then he says, 'Mini here can drop the phat beat.'"

Of all the bizarre people we'd met in Chicago, this had finally crossed the line into absurdity.

When I was in high school, there were twelve of us girls who "ran together." I generally hated when adults used that phrase to describe a group of adolescents, but in our case the phrase was accurate. We were known as "the Clan"—(that's Clan with a "C"). A fellow student dubbed us the Clan our freshman year, and teachers and students alike started to use it. We were a loud, obnoxious bunch—half of us were cheerleaders, and the other half had no excuse. Other students complained that we were an "exclusive clique." We didn't mean to exclude others. The main problem was that we had our own unique subculture—our own language, norms, and sanctions. Outsiders could not thrive.

Teachers tried to temper our overwhelming presence with lectures about how we needed to be more inclusive. Our principal went so far as to pull us out of class one day to say, "I'm worried that the Clan has all the makings of a gang." We were twelve high-school girls who shopped at American Eagle and talked mostly about classes and cheerleading. I didn't exactly envision us turning our school into the next Compton anytime soon.

The Clan's weekend entertainment was a collectively acquired taste as well. Friday night activities might include seeing how many of us we could pack into one car, using weird accents to order at fast-food drive-through windows, and running around a grocery store with sheets over our heads until we got kicked out.

If someone were to eavesdrop on one of our slumber parties, they wouldn't have been able to understand a word we said. The twelve of us had years of history together, and we had a name for everything that had ever happened to us. We even had a name for each of our all-Clan fights so we could easily reference them after the fact—as in "Didn't you side with me during the Fight in the Park?" or "I swore she agreed with me about that before the Great Schism."

The "All-Night Fight," one of our bigger fights, pitted the six cheerleaders against the six non-cheerleaders in a yelling match from eight at night until six thirty the following morning. "You guys leave us out!" the non-cheerleaders accused. "You guys have inside jokes we don't understand!" they yelled. Poof! They had unleashed the ace in the hole. The Clan had hundreds of inside jokes *together* as a unit, but group norms forbade small factions of the Clan from developing their *own* inside jokes.

We finished the All-Night Fight just as the sun came up with a big group hug and forgiving promises that all would return to normal. The cheerleaders then decided to go to sleep, but the non-cheerleaders wanted to first make blueberry pancakes for breakfast before going to bed. Just to have the last word, Brittany, a cheerleader who was trying to sleep, called out to the girls in the kitchen, "Your blueberry pancakes smell like vomit!" The comment made all the cheerleaders laugh hysterically. The non-cheerleaders did not. But regardless of raw nerves or residual bitterness, the Clan would always remain the Clan. Years of shared history is a cord not easily unbound.

Urban families were good replacements for traditional families, but they weren't the same as being part of a Clan. It was understood that an urban family was based on very loose ties that would eventually be severed after people moved on to new stages of life and went their separate ways. The makeup of an urban family involved a mix of too many different backgrounds, beliefs, and future dreams to have a chance for long-term survival. Unlike the Clan, there was no shared history to bind the group together through time and change. Perhaps the transient tendencies of urban families contributed to a certain underlying sadness permeating the city.

On *Leave It to Beaver*, Eddie Haskell always said he was going to "give someone the business." So it was Eddie's face that popped into my mind at The Bar one night when I overheard Kenya telling Scott, "The business is really changing my life" and "The business is better than I ever thought it would be."

Hunter had forewarned me that their roommate Kenya was involved in a multilevel marketing scheme, but that didn't stop me from asking her to tell me more about "the business."

"You should just come to a meeting with me this week," Kenya said.

I didn't know Kenya all that well. I only knew she lived with the guys and wasn't around very much because she had a boyfriend in Milwaukee with whom she stayed on weekends.

"I don't think I necessarily need to go to a meeting," I told her.

"The best way for you to learn about the business is to come and see it for yourself," Kenya said. "Mark's already coming with me this week. Do you work on Sunday night?"

"No, but I ..."

"Just share a cab with Mark then," Kenya said. "I'm telling you, this meeting could change your life."

I figured if nothing else, going to Kenya's "business meeting" would give me a chance to view firsthand all the classic persuasion techniques I had learned in social psychology. When Mark and I entered the hotel ballroom where the meeting was taking place, upbeat motivational music was playing and friendly, well-dressed people greeted us. Coffee and cookies were set up on a long table in the back of the room. (*When people are in a positive mood, they are more susceptible to persuasion.*)

"Are you new?" a woman asked me. She told me she had only been in the business for about a month. "It's the best thing that's ever happened to me," she said. "My brother got me involved, and now we're trying to convince our parents to join up too." When I asked her for more details about the business itself, she said, "The president will clear up all your questions in the meeting." Mark got cornered by a large, jovial woman who told him, "I really can't explain to you what the business has done for me." Tears formed in her eyes. "I have this freedom I didn't have before, you know?"

Kenya introduced us to the president of the business, Ron Reynolds. Ron was a handsome man, and he stood with his arm around his beautiful wife, Leah. They were both proverbially "down-to-earth," an ambiguous and overused expression I typically like to avoid—except in this case, the description was all that seemed to work. I instantly liked them both. (*The message will be more widely accepted if the communicator is somewhat attractive and has a generally likable personality.)* Ron spoke quickly and confidently, telling us how happy he was that we had decided to accept Kenya's invitation and come to a meeting. *(People who speak faster come across as more credible than people who speak slower.)*

As we took our seats, Mark and I exchanged a couple of jokes about making sure not to drink any Kool-Aid. I couldn't believe how quickly the room had filled up, but I looked around and estimated there were at least two hundred people present. *(The bigger the group, the more likely it is that the people will conform to whatever is being asked of them.)*

Ron opened by saying, "Today is the first day of the rest of your life!" The room erupted in claps and cheers. The business, we soon learned, involved selling specific products that had become increasingly valued in the international marketplace. But, as expected, the main thrust of the business was recruiting friends and neighbors to sell the products along with you.

Ron said, "I was once just like you, sitting there and thinking that this whole thing sounded like one big pyramid scheme. But I can assure you 100 percent that it is not." *(Skeptical people are more easily persuaded by a two-sided message as opposed to a one-sided message. A two-sided message is when you acknowledge any opposing arguments to your message and then attempt to refute them.)*

"If you don't get involved in the business today," Ron said, "I can tell you that you will be missing out on one of the greatest opportunities of a lifetime." *(People respond quicker to the fear of losing out on something than the hope of gaining something.)*

"Raise your hand if this business has changed the way you live!" Ron yelled. Hands flew up all around me. There were more claps and cheers. "If you want to be successful in every area of your life, you must keep company with people who have already experienced the success you are seeking. You must be willing to risk trading an ordinary life for an extraordinary life. I am confident that you are the kind of people who can see the long-term benefits of taking that risk. You are the kind of people who are willing to take risks when other people sit back and say it can't be done!" *(An effective persuader can nudge people into a desired course of action by convincing them they are the "sort of people" who engage in this type of activity.)*

Several people stood and gave brief testimonials about how much money they had made through the business and how it had changed their lives. During the final testimony, soft background music began to play: "*Right now. Hey, it's your tomorrow ...*" Ron asked a group of men in expensive suits and matching red ties to hand out "contracts" to all the new people in the crowd. "This is the real deal, folks," Ron said. "This is it ... this is your moment."

Neither Mark nor I had made a wisecrack in quite a while; we were both listening intently. "The contract you're being handed is *your ticket* into our family," Ron said. "We are a group of people who have the same intelligence, the same drive, the same integrity, and the same goals that you have. Signing this contract is your first step toward becoming one of us, and we are in this for the long haul. You heard some of the testimonies tonight ... people have been in the business for ten, fifteen, even twenty-five years. We've been here for each other through all that time, and we'll keep being here." The crowd erupted.

"All you have to do is make a small investment of $750. That money will be repaid to you in full as soon as you are able to get three more people involved with the business—which should be easy to do because you'll have plenty of support along the way with everyone at your side cheering you on. A mere $750 is nothing for a lifetime of opportunity, growth, wealth, and, most importantly, friendship."

I couldn't believe it, but I was considering joining the business. I knew it was a pyramid scheme. I knew it was ludicrous, but I still wanted to belong to this group of people. They were happy and excited; they knew what they wanted. They had a plan in life, and I obviously didn't.

"After you recoup your initial investment, your network will continue to grow," Ron said. "Then one day you, like me, will be able to say, 'I made my millions because I went with my heart and took the advice of some guy I first thought was crazy!'"

"Are you guys in?" Kenya whispered to us. I guessed she had yet to recoup her original $750 investment. Ron was asking for anyone who signed the contract to bring it down front and place it on the stairs of the platform. "This is a public act to show you're serious about becoming one of us," he said. At least fifty people broke away from the confining rows of chairs and freely jammed the aisles. I wondered if any of them were planted in the audience to create an even greater sense of peer pressure. That thought led me to wonder if the two women Mark and I had met at the beginning of the meeting had also been planted. Yet, even as I thought about these things, I still wanted to go forward. What had gotten into me? *(We grossly underestimate the inherent power of a situation to shape our behavior. We believe the power of the individual can act independently of situational forces because we must believe we have control over our own lives. But this is called the fundamental attribution error, because the power of the situation has a far greater pull on us than we may think.)*

"Kenya, could I sleep on it?" I asked.

Mark firmly clamped his hand on my arm. "Can we *please* get out of here now?" he asked.

As soon as I breathed in the fresh night air, my common sense returned.

"I almost signed up," I told Mark as we walked to hail a cab.

"You did not," he said.

"I swear I almost did."

"But that was one of the most blatant pyramid schemes I've ever heard of," Mark said.

"All Ron's motivational crap got to me though ..." I admitted.

"You are losing it."

I knew things were bad if the Grim Reaper had to tell me that

I was the crazy one.

"It would just be nice to be part of a group," I said.

"What do you think the restaurant is?" he asked.

"Yeah, but I'm talking about a group that will still be around years from now," I said.

"You think too much about the future. That's why I keep telling you to concentrate more on the moment. Besides, just because something's still around years from now doesn't make it superior to something that's not," Mark said.

I slid into the cab and changed the subject to Zulu.

The best antidote to Haley, a pure-bred midwestern Trixie, was Nola, an angry Polish lesbian. I had expected there would be a token homosexual in any urban work setting I found myself in, but I imagined the person would be a *he*—a fun-loving, overly feminine gay man with superb style and a loud laugh. This was not to be at Paronelli's. Nola's overall demeanor was far more masculine than most men I knew. When she shot other servers a look of disgust after they screwed up an order, they would shiver and cower in fear.

Nola had a girlfriend of two years named Jade. Her pet name for Jade was "the ultimate lesbian butch." Sometimes she swapped the *u* in butch for an *i*, depending on how well she and Jade were getting along. I couldn't imagine that anyone besides Nola herself could hold the ULB title.

"How's Jade been?" I asked Nola.

"Don't ask," Nola said. "Things are complicated right now."

It seemed like "things" had become increasingly complicated lately. Nola wanted to adopt a child, but Jade wasn't ready. Jade wanted a formal commitment, but Nola didn't think that was necessary. Jade's parents didn't get along with Nola; Nola's mom didn't know about Jade.

"Are you making any trips to Poland to see your mom this year?" I asked.

"No," Nola said.

Nola was a woman of few words. She rarely talked to customers, and she only offered limited small talk to servers. When she got angry with someone, however, she let the person know, occasionally in a way that involved the police (or so we had heard). To her credit, she was a hard worker, and she tried to stay out of the Paronelli's drama whenever possible. "Everybody here is so immature and stupid," she would say in her think Polish accent.

Nola was an activist in the Chicago gay and lesbian community, so she was the obvious server of choice for the GLBT crowd. Hunter had named one of her regulars "Bug Boy" because his eyes sort of bugged out of his head—an expression that, to me, made very little sense the more I thought about it. Nonetheless, Bug Boy did manage to bug every single server at Paronelli's by constantly touting the benefits of sensory-deprivation tanks. He once talked to Brad about them for two hours straight. The whole thing sounded very weird to me, but Bug Boy insisted that being enclosed in a sensory-deprivation tank was the closest he'd ever come to enlightenment.

Bug Boy had a weird accent, and when I inquired about where he was from, he told me Transylvania. He also told me his parents were vampires, and he went into detail about how they stored vials of blood in their kitchen refrigerator. He talked about assorted vampire rituals he had seen and how he was finally able to escape from such a terrible family life and move to the States. A few months later, Bug Boy told me that all the vampire lore he had shared with me had been a big joke. He was actually from North Dakota. His dad was a teacher, and his mom a dental hygienist.

Bug Boy and his boyfriend Stanley came in every Thursday night to see Nola. Stanley was the fun-loving, stylish gay man I had imagined I would work alongside, pre-Nola. He even had a laugh so loud that I could tell the moment he entered the restaurant. He made jokes just so he could laugh at himself.

"We boys love Nola," Stanley would say, "but we definitely don't screw with her!"

Nola's younger sister was bipolar. When she was nineteen, she shot and killed their stepfather. Eight years later, she was still in prison. Nola's mother never fully recovered from the trauma and had recently attempted suicide. She had failed and was now living in a supervised group home in Poland.

The gay and lesbian community of Chicago had been an excellent substitute for Nola's nonexistent nuclear family. Nola lived in an area of Lakeview sometimes called Boystown. The rainbow pillar-laden street of North Halstead offered anything a person could ever want or need, but with a gay flair. Nola could shop at Gay Mart or party at Club Uranus. The stores were full of sex toys, and the bars were full of transvestites.

By living in Boystown, Nola could ensure that every friend she made would be gay, and she could begin her new family with her lesbian partner while frequenting and supporting only GLBT-owned, or at least GLBT-friendly, businesses.

Although Nola said very little to her coworkers, she loved to gab with her regulars—her friends and neighbors from Boystown. Every time I eavesdropped on those conversations, I found them riddled with sexual innuendoes and consisting of precious little aside from discussions of sex lives and sexual identity.

I had heard other regulars from the gay and lesbian community complain, "Sex isn't the only thing that defines us! We have so many other interests." I knew they were right; they did have numerous other interests. But sex just happened to be one of the most important ones.

The definition of religion is "a cause, a principle, or an activity pursued with zeal and a conscientious devotion." Sexuality was Nola's religion.

Nola had studied psychology at Loyola. When I asked her what she had planned to do with her degree, she said, "One of these days, I'm going to sit down and sort out all my own [stuff]."

"Do you ever want to counsel other people?" I asked.

"Are you kidding?" Nola said in disbelief. I might as well have asked her if she ever wanted to become straight.

"Newsflash ..." Nola said, "I've actually seen some disturbing things in my life. I could never sit for eight hours a day and listen to dramatic little people talk about petty little problems from their stupid little lives."

I understood. Most therapists end up listening to girls like Haley who can afford the weekly visits. Nola couldn't handle five minutes of Haley whining about Jackson, let alone fifty minutes. Often if Haley even opened her mouth to speak one sentence to Nola during their Sunday afternoon shift, Nola would instantly put up a hand to silence her.

"Do you think you'll ever get a psych-related job?" I asked.

"Come on." Nola sounded irritated. "You think I'm going to let all that money spent on an education count for nothing?"

I shrugged. Isn't that what most of us had done?

"I'll eventually get my PhD," she continued. "Then I'll be able to conduct research that will support GLBT causes ... since that's really the only cause in this world that matters."

It began slowly.

First, I didn't do a double-take when I saw two boys holding hands walking down Broadway.

Next, a notoriously gay reality-TV star came into Paronelli's, and I drew straws with Haley to see who would get the honor of waiting on him.

Then, I laughed after I excused myself to go to the bathroom in a restaurant near Boystown, and I found that the signs on the restroom doors read "Queens" and "Queers."

Finally, I almost felt guilty for hanging out with any group of people that wasn't diverse enough to include at least one homosexual.

I was policing my own free time to ensure political correctness, even though it was a lifestyle I didn't agree with.

Desensitization: to make emotionally unresponsive as by long exposure to repeated shocks.

I read that historians can point out specific characteristics that have manifested in every major civilization in history *just before* that civilization met its final destruction. It's as though there are some specific warning signs to alert an empire of its imminent fall. One of those warning signs is the rampant spread and embracing of homosexuality.

I knew that some people might chalk up Nola's sexual preferences to her unfortunate family situation. But a bad background was no longer a prerequisite for an alternative lifestyle. The media has made sure of that by going to great lengths to impress upon the minds of a generation that experimentation is ultra chic. MTV and the like have so thoroughly confused millions of youth, that now every time a high-school kid feels *any* emotion for *any* person, he or she is stupid enough to sit down and ponder what that might mean with regard to his or her sexuality. If a girl has a fun time hanging out with a female friend, or if a guy admires the quarterback of the football team, rather than recognize that not every emotion is supposed to be translated into sexual expression, those kids would stop to ponder the meaning of their reactions. In this way, they partially stop seeing the people around them as whole beings with minds and souls, and instead, value them as physical bodies and little more.

"Why don't Nola and Jade ever come to The Bar?" I asked Mark as Kyle set our drinks in front of us.

"Those two in a straight bar?" Kyle jumped in. "Not a chance."

"He's right," Mark said. "There's no way they'd ever feel comfortable in a place like this. And could you really blame them?" He nodded toward the three cowboy regulars sitting near the window.

"Last week," Kyle said, "one of my older customers told me, 'Kyle, I hope you never serve drinks to them gays. 'Cause if you're dumb enough to serve 'em, you're dumb enough to be one of 'em.'"

Mark laughed. "I can't believe how homophobic some people can be."

"It's all because of those crazy fundamentalist churches," Kyle said.

"But why do those churches think someone like Nola, who doesn't believe in God in the first place, is going to care about what God supposedly has to say?" Mark asked.

"That's beside the point," Kyle said. "The fact is that no one can tell someone else whom they can or can't love."

"That's true," I said. "But you can tell people how they can and can't express that love, which is why no one questions our laws against pedophiles. Just because you feel something for someone doesn't mean it's okay to express it sexually."

"Your argument holds no weight because we're talking about two consenting, non-related adults here," Mark said.

"There are a lot of things two non-related adults can both consent to do—from robbing a bank to having an affair—but it still doesn't make it right," I said.

"So basically, you're telling me the government should legislate morality?" Mark asked.

"No," I said. I didn't want to dig myself into the grave of "narrow-minded, right-wing zealot" yet again. "Never mind."

"Hey, it's cool," Kyle said. "You can give your opinion. You know Mark and I aren't the kind of guys who will badmouth you behind your back for disagreeing with us. We like people who think for themselves."

For the first time, it was actually safe to share my opinion. Unfortunately, I couldn't think of anything intelligent to say.

I remember reading Romans 1:18-29 in the Bible, which says,

> The wrath of God is being revealed from heaven against all the godlessness and wickedness of men who suppress the truth by their wickedness, since what may be known about God is plain to them, because God has made it plain to them. For since the creation of the world God's invisible qualities—his eternal power and divine nature—have been clearly seen, being understood from what has been made, so that men are without excuse. For although they knew God, they neither glorified him as

God nor gave thanks to him, but their thinking became futile and their foolish hearts were darkened ... Therefore God gave them over in the sinful desires of their hearts to sexual impurity for the degrading of their bodies with one another. They exchanged the truth of God for a lie, and worshiped and served created things rather than the Creator—who is forever praised. Amen. Because of this, God gave them over to shameful lusts. Even their women exchanged natural relations for unnatural ones. In the same way the men also abandoned natural relations with women and were inflamed with lust for one another. Men committed indecent acts with other men ... [God] gave them over to a depraved mind, to do what ought not to be done. They have become filled with every kind of wickedness. (NIV)

Verses like these made me question why so many churches were wasting time debating God's view of homosexuality.

Jordan was sitting on a stool next to Mark and me, deep in conversation with a Bar regular about some band with a name so absurd that it made me want to curse the night they smoked weed and came up with it. I'm talking about an utterly ridiculous name with six-plus words strung together simply *because* they sounded absolutely insane together. Something like Fat Kinsey and the Slaughterhouse Cactus or Origami Pineapples, Sex, Soy, and Sorrow. And their name was probably the very reason they would always and forever remain a local band.

I turned and joined in Jordan's conversation anyway, just to avoid further debate on homosexuality.

"So this band might start opening for us," Jordan said. "Us" meaning Sidewalks in Hell, which I had long ago decided to be an acceptable band name. After all, it was only three words in length, *and* it evoked a tangible mental image. The second qualification was the key because sticking to three words or fewer didn't exonerate a band from sounding like a freak show, (case in point: Paper Sandbox Catastrophe, Rabbit's Lithuanian Theory, or Green Toothbrush Army). If the band's name had some meaning—any meaning—it passed the test. So Three Doors Down and Crash Test Dummies would make the cut, but Alien Ant Farm and Stone Temple Pilots would not.

"Hunter and I are still arguing over whether or not to let them open for us starting next month," Jordan said. I didn't bother asking Jordan to repeat the band's name because I knew hearing something like Uncle Hummus Meet the Eucalyptus Planet would make me sick to my stomach.

"You know who the band's lead singer is, right?" Jordan asked me. "It's Silas, the guy who comes into Paronelli's and always orders a caesar salad without croutons."

"Yeah, I know who you're talking about," I said. "He's the guy who looks like he's ..." I stopped myself mid-sentence because I didn't want to be classified as homophobic. "The guy who's so skinny he looks like he's a heroin addict, and he owns, like, thirty multicolored scarves that he wears in a rotation when it gets cold."

"That's him," Jordan said. "Silas Sanders the Scarf Specialist, from Saint Charles, Missouri. But if you decide to call him by his full title, he prefers you leave off Missouri for effect."

"I'll keep that in mind," I said.

"Oh, and just in case you were wondering, Silas *isn't* gay," Jordan said. "But he *is* a heroin addict."

That explained the wretched band name.

"Hey, Jordan," Mark interrupted. "Screw Silas Sanders ... we were actually in the middle of a real conversation about serious issues over here, so enough talk about some lame opening band."

"That's pretty sick, Mark," Jordan said. "I never knew you wanted to screw Silas Sanders."

"Okay, I just ate dinner," Mark said. "And I had Mario's ravioli with gorgonzola sauce. So unless you want to see that ravioli on this floor right now, please don't say something like that ever again." Mark's reaction was ideal. For a thirteen-year-old.

"Mark," Kyle said, "didn't you just say about a minute ago that you can't believe how homophobic some people are?" We all laughed.

"I admit it, Kyle," Mark said. "You got me on that one, man." He made no further excuses for his double standard.

I never understood what homosexuals visualized when they heard the word "homophobic"—until I attended the Chicago Gay Pride Parade. The lavish costumes and floats full of half-naked people with no definable sex did not draw the most raised eyebrows that day; rather, the "Christian" protesters did. They carried signs that read, "Sodomy is to die for," "No parking in rear," and the old standby, "Adam and Eve, not Adam and Steve." They shouted through large bullhorns as the parade passed by: "The wages of sin is death!" "Your body and soul will burn in hell!"

After about an hour of this, a group of boys in rainbow T-shirts who were riding on a parade float walked over to them. The boys formed a line in front of the mob and got down on their knees. Bystanders wondered if they were getting ready to make a collective rude gesture, as several parade marchers had already done. But as we watched, the line of boys silently folded their hands, closed their eyes ... and started to pray for the protestors.

TEN

THE
REAL
WORLD

"A man's true wealth is the good he does in this world."
—Mohammed

"I need to tell you something," Rachel said.

Her tone was too serious for a Dunkin' Donuts conversation, and it worried me. She wasn't making eye contact with me either. She was twirling her finger in the whipped cream on top of her Mocha Blast, staring intently at the pattern she was creating. "I'm moving home in three days," she said.

"You're what?" I was in shock.

"This weekend is the only weekend my brother can come to Chicago to help me move," she explained. "I need to go home. I'm so sick of working at the Gap, and I'm tired of all the Landons, Er Ders, and Mini Kahns I keep getting involved with. I'm just *over* the whole city thing."

I agreed that it would be nice to resume a life among the sane, but I thought moving home in *three* days was a bit extreme.

Rachel begged me not to be angry with her. Too late. I was angry that she was leaving me all alone, and I was angry that an event I had no power over was going to permanently affect me.

"Me moving home isn't going to change your life here that much," Rachel said.

A hundred questions marched single-file through my head. "What about our lease?" I asked.

"I already explained our situation to Dan," Rachel said. "He said you can finish out the month we've already paid for, and then he'll let us out of our lease. So you'll just have to find your own place after that."

Rachel knew I couldn't afford a studio apartment.

"I'm *so* sorry," she said. "Do you hate me?"

I said nothing.

Three days later, I waved goodbye to Rachel from the doorway of our building. Honks from angry drivers filled the air as Rachel's brother clumsily maneuvered his truck packed with her belongings out of its parking space. I walked back into our now eerily silent apartment. It was 5:43 p.m., and I had to go to work ... I didn't have time to break down.

Abu was often overlooked at Paronelli's because he was "just the delivery guy." He was usually only around the restaurant at the beginning of our six o'clock shift and at the end, just before we closed. In between, he carted covered plates of pasta to the homes of lazy Lincoln Park residents. Abu was a stout African American with a warm personality and a deep devotion to Islam.

Abu's most noticeable attribute was his walk. He walked very, very slowly everywhere he went. It was fortunate for him that Paronelli's owned a delivery truck. If he had to deliver orders by foot, his unhurried gait might have cost him his job. Nonetheless, he was one of the more charming and friendly Paronelli's employees.

"Brad told me about Rachel just up and leaving you like that," Abu said as he gathered up his deliveries to begin his route. "What are you going to do after your lease is up?"

"I don't know ..." I knew the decision could be detrimental to my future, which is why I didn't even want to think about it. I desperately wanted another Dr. Porter-like experience where someone else gave me the words that pushed me in the right direction.

"Don't even *think* about leaving us," Abu said in a stern, fatherly tone. "This place wouldn't be the same without you here."

I knew Abu was wrong. If I left, Mr. Paronelli would put up the Help Wanted sign as he had forewarned, and a new server would take my place within hours. But no matter how exaggerated Abu's words might be, they still managed to nullify Mr. Paronelli's words to me long ago—"Always remember how dispensable you are." Abu's compliment reminded me that although Rachel might soon be thousands of miles away, I had been wrong about one thing— she hadn't really left me all alone in the city after all.

It was ten thirty at night, and Maxwell, one of my favorite regulars, was the only person in the restaurant. Maxwell came in every night at ten for a caprese salad and a piece of chocolate cheesecake. He was born in Africa, grew up in France, went to college in Italy, and had been working in the States for seven years. He spoke English, Spanish, French, Italian, and a tribal dialect he learned as a young boy. He said his grandmother had been a sage. Apparently, she read palms with such accuracy that important political figures in Africa flew her to their homes to reveal their future. Maxwell said he'd inherited his grandmother's gift for supernatural intuition. I occasionally saw him read a customer's palm.

"I'll go ahead and order the usual tonight," Maxwell called to me from the end of the bar.

"You want coffee too?" I asked.

"No," he said, then paused and smiled. "By the way, you're going to find your one true love."

"Excuse me?"

"You're going to find your one true love. I can feel it."

This was hardly the type of sign I had been hoping for. I wasn't going to stay in the city because a self-proclaimed sage thought I might find true love. Romance had not been a top priority for me in a long time. I had never been one to obsess over finding a soul mate. Not since I was about ten and in love with Ryan, anyway.

"What do you mean?" I asked.

"I already said exactly what I meant," he winked. "That's all I can say."

By the time I brought Maxwell his salad, he was speaking rapid Spanish, in the middle of an intense conversation with Mario. I poured myself a Coke and sat at the bar, opening the *Tribune* in front of me. Brad had let Haley go home early, and he was now in the office "taking care of an accounting issue." I had a hunch that the wafting smell of incense might soon permeate the restaurant.

"How'd deliveries go tonight?" I asked Abu.

"There was a little mix-up," he said. "Leslie Olsen accidentally got a pasta dish with sausage *and* mozzarella in it."

"Oops," I said, knowing Leslie was a vegan.

"So, I forget," Abu said. "Did I tell you I finally decided I'm going to do this thing in a couple weeks?"

"This thing" was a reference to Abu's upcoming prearranged marriage. Abu was in his fifties and had already been married and divorced three times. He wanted to try a different approach the fourth time around, so he asked his family to pick out his next bride. They chose a nice Muslim girl from California whose parents had been longtime family friends. Although Abu had never seen his future bride, he was going to drive to San Diego to meet and marry her in the same day.

Abu had two children who more or less parted ways with him after he went to prison for ten years on an armed robbery charge. But that all happened before he changed his life and returned to his Islamic roots while behind bars. He had been making an honest living ever since he got paroled thirteen years ago.

"How much do you know about this girl?" I asked.

"She seems nice in her letters," Abu said. "And she's real pretty in the pictures I've seen."

"How much does she know about you?" I asked. (My subtext was, "Does she know you're an ex-con?")

Abu read my mind. "Well, I finally told her I'd been in lockup for a little bit," he said.

I personally didn't consider a decade a "little bit," but whatever.

Abu glanced down at the headline of the *Tribune* article I was reading.

"This Middle East stuff is out of control," he said. "It's such a shame because Muslims and Christians both worship Allah." I wasn't sure if I agreed.

"Don't Muslims think that if a person refuses to believe that Mohammed is Allah's prophet, that person goes to hell?"

"No, no, no, no," Abu said. "There are passages in the Qur'an that say both Christians and Jews can get into paradise. Abraham gave birth to Ishmael, who later settled in Mecca. But he also gave birth to Isaac, whose bloodline formed the twelve tribes of Israel. So we're all related."

Abu went on to talk about how much he respected the prophets, including Mohammed and Jesus Christ.

"The Qur'an says human beings are always forgetting the very thing that should be our ultimate concern in life," Abu said. "Specifically the day of judgment, which is coming whether we believe it is or not."

Abu explained that the Qur'an repeatedly determines itself as a reminder to humanity that the true definition of success is entry into paradise in the afterlife.

"Is it true that the name Allah is whispered to every newborn Muslim baby and to every dying Muslim man?" I asked.

"Yep," Abu said. "It's the first word people hear when they enter the world and the last word they hear before leaving it."

"That's a beautiful practice," I said.

"I was thinking on my delivery route tonight," Abu said. "Why don't I plan my trip to California so that I leave on the day your lease is up? That way you can live rent-free in my place for the three weeks I'm gone, and it'll buy you a little more time to figure out what to do next. Then you won't make a rash decision like Rachel did."

It wasn't a bad idea.

"I have to go back to the office and give my delivery report to Brad," Abu said. "But I want you to seriously consider my proposal."

Abu took nearly thirty minutes to walk the length of the bar back to Brad's office, even though it should have been about an eight-second trek. He took so long because he stopped to tend to any obstacle en route to his final destination. He stopped to talk to the cooks. He stopped to study the entertainment section of the *Chicago Reader* that was lying on the floor. He stopped to examine a few new scuffs on his left shoe. He stopped to retrace his steps, looking for a receipt he thought he had dropped, only to eventually find it in his pocket where it belonged. Abu probably had ADD, but after his kind offer and all the nice things he had said to me, I found his nuances to be tolerable, if not endearing.

Living at Abu's for three weeks meant I had to step over a prayer rug every night on my way to the bathroom. But his apartment was cozy, and I slept well on the big leather couch. Without Rachel at home to talk to, I soon became one of "those people" who spent all their free time hanging out at Paronelli's and The Bar. Kyle's deep, gruff smoker's voice greeted me each night. "What's new at your place, you little Jihad warrior?" Kyle's voice didn't conjure up images of lung cancer and early death; instead, women were always telling him, "I wish every man's voice sounded exactly like yours." Despite his notable vocal chords, Kyle himself was short and rather unobtrusive. He had dark bed-head hair and dark eyes. His smile revealed deep dimples and teeth far straighter and whiter than most Trixies.

I was impressed with Kyle's social skills from the moment we met. Everyone in Chicago was eager to tell me his or her story, but Kyle was the first person to ask me about mine. He expressed genuine interest in everything I said—and not in an I'd-like-to-score-a-date-with-you kind of way, but in a real-life, I'm-a-bartender-you-can-tell-me-anything kind of way.

Kyle had a degree in creative writing, and he wanted to move to Hollywood to become a screenwriter. He struck me as too smart for the whole "move to Hollywood and chase fame" thing, but at least he wanted to write films rather than act in them. Kyle loved talking about movies, and we bonded over our mutual respect for Mark Borchardt from *American Movie*. We expressed solidarity over which other movies were worth watching as well, from our favorite foreign film, *Life Is Beautiful*, to our favorite blockbuster, *The Lord of the Rings*.

We were surprised to learn we had attended colleges that were a mere fifteen miles apart. When we discovered we had three mutual friends, I refrained from remarking "small world," and instead thought about the fact that it really kind of was. There I sat, in a bar in Chicago, talking to a person I had just narrowly missed meeting many times before in prior years.

Kyle had been bartending ever since he graduated from college. But even though Scott and the other bartenders pounded back countless shots with regulars, Kyle rarely drank when he worked. He once told me, "Alcohol never made anyone a better person."

Scott was a clean-cut frat boy who reminded me of someone famous, but I couldn't put my finger on whom, and it annoyed me. Scott used to be a server at Paronelli's until he got fired for a mishap involving pyrotechnics. He was still bitter about his termination. Even though it had been more than a year, he continued to boycott Paronelli's. Scott had his master of business and had a brief stint as a day trader downtown while still in grad school. He watched CNN for up-to-the-minute news and then bought and sold stocks according to the market's response to international events. When Scott realized he was making far more money bartending than he was trading, he quit the business world to bartend full time.

"I have a question," Scott said, sliding me a dish of pretzels across the bar. "Who's better looking—me or Kyle? Be honest." I was too dumbstruck by his question to formulate a witty response.

"You don't even have to tell me," Scott said. "I already know the answer is Kyle because Kyle gets *all* the girls." Scott's feigned-humility tactic was one of many tools he used to garner female attention. He wanted my response to be "Whatever, Scott, there are *so many* girls who like you!" which I wasn't about to say, even though at least five of those girls were within my peripheral vision at the bar.

Scott had realized he could wield a great deal of power by never romantically committing to anyone, so he hadn't dated any girl exclusively in seven years. That didn't stop him, however, from flirting with and leading on every female in a tri-state radius. His elusive "I don't date" persona made him appear far more complicated and mysterious than he actually was. His constant need for female attention was astounding.

"No, seriously," Scott said (although I knew he wasn't serious), "what is it with all these girls and Kyle? I mean, there must be some good qualities about me, right?" He continued to bait the line, but I wasn't biting.

"Actually," I said, "the only good quality about you is that you're friends with Kyle." It was kind of true. Scott threw a pretzel at me, but he missed because his gaze had wandered mid-throw to the front door of The Bar, where several employees from Mexicana Fiesta, a restaurant down the street, had just walked in.

"Pedro!" Scott shouted. "Dawg, where you been all my life?" Scott leaped over the bar so he could hug the incoming customers.

Our conversation was over as quickly as it had begun. Scott was one of those people who loved to work the room. He was the ultimate sanguine personality and had far more acquaintances than friends. Each girl he met felt special because of the intense attention Scott bestowed upon her. Unfortunately, he gave the same concentrated attention to everyone he knew—before quickly moving on to the next person. Still, each girl believed she might be the one to break Scott from his pattern of non-committal "player" status. But, protected from all vulnerability, Scott remained in control of his life and left a disgruntled group of jilted would-be girlfriends in his wake.

Scott's large female following was somewhat surprising, considering he used pickup lines like "I used to be a day trader. Wanna trade numbers?" Kyle thought that Scott, former Mr. Day Trader himself, would one day realize that the best trade he could make would be to trade in the admiration of many for the intimacy of one.

"Yo, dawg, you *need* to tell that little mamacita Rosalita to come in and see me ASAP," Scott said, with a pat to Pedro's back.

I didn't see that trade coming anytime soon.

"So, Miss Mohammed," Kyle said, "don't you have to be out of Abu's place by next week?"

"Why do you keep reminding me?" I asked. "You know I have nowhere to go when I move out."

"Did Hunter and Jordan tell you about Kenya?" Kyle asked.

"No," I said. "But I try not to get involved in Kenya's business." I smiled at my clever pun.

"Well, Kenya and her business up and moved to Milwaukee last week without even saying goodbye," Kyle said. "I guess she and her boyfriend just bought a house there."

"No way," I said. "Good for her, though; she needed a change."

"So, I was thinking," Kyle said, "if you want Kenya's old room, it's yours."

"Get real," I said. "You guys pay $5,600 a month in rent. You know I could never afford that."

"You wouldn't have to pay rent," Kyle said. "You could live rent-free if you just helped out with utilities."

"Yeah right," I said, "like Hunter and Jordan would *ever* agree to that."

"I *guarantee* they will," Kyle said. "Just let me take care of it."

I felt like the ultimate vagabond even considering such an offer, but I couldn't deny the coincidental timing.

Kyle "took care of it" by telling Hunter and Jordan he'd erase their tab at The Bar if they let me move in for a while. Their tab was no small number. I moved in two days later.

My new apartment defined "location, location, location." It was perched atop a popular live music venue on one of the busiest streets in the north side of Chicago. Some of the best jazz and Mediterranean cuisine was literally right next door. The apartment itself had six bedrooms, three bathrooms, and one long spiral staircase cutting through its two levels. On each level, enormous round windows provided ample sunlight, and the private roof deck had a spectacular cityscape view.

But for every pro there was a con, and the apartment was far from perfect. Jordan had made a fort in the living room using hundreds of empty pizza boxes. Scott and Kenya had wallpapered the dining room with junk mail. The living room couches were green-striped monstrosities full of holes and dark beer stains. And the kitchen belonged on a talk-show special about people with hoarding disorders. At least I shared a bathroom with neat-freak Bria. Ours was the only one that had been cleaned in two years.

Hunter's bedroom consisted of a bare mattress on the floor, a couple Sidewalks in Hell posters on the walls, and piles of clothes up to four feet high in some corners. Kyle's room looked a lot like Hunter's, except he owned a down comforter and had posters of jazz legends on his walls. Scott's room was littered in *Fast Company* magazines and other business paraphernalia, although he actually had a desk with a computer on it.

Bria usually kept her door shut, and I had never been inside her room. But I knew she had her own TV because she never watched TV in the living room with the rest of us. And I knew she had a nice stereo because I could hear Indigo Girls songs coming from her room each morning. I always liked the line they sang, "The less I seek my source for some definitive, the closer I am to fine." There was no doubt in my mind that the Indigo Girls were right. The less I bothered to seek out truth, the less I was troubled by all the questions that accompanied the search. Ignorance was bliss. But ignorance was still ignorance.

Jordan's room was my favorite. His floor was littered with hundreds of DVDs—an investment that could have easily bought a hot meal for every beggar in Chicago. Oddly enough, Jordan had no bed. He slept in a sleeping bag inside a pop-up tent in the middle of his room. On his otherwise bare walls hung an enormous AC/DC poster proclaiming in large letters, "Lock Up Your Daughters." It was the sentence that best summed up what every parent needed to know regarding Jordan.

The day I moved in, Scott jokingly said, "You're probably only moving in here so you can write some exposé article about all of us for the *Reader*."

"You caught me," I said. "But why write an article about you guys when I could write a book instead?"

He laughed.

My new bedroom was directly over the stage of the venue below us, which had live music six nights a week. Neil Diamond cover songs lullabied me to sleep. Living with Hunter and Jordan, I finally got to see their disgusting habits up close. True to form, they brought home a new groupie each weekend, and there was no end to their alcoholism. I walked into the apartment at three in the afternoon on Saint Patty's Day and found Jordan passed out in fetal position on the kitchen tile. Hunter came home from The Bar one night and, barely coherent, asked me to cover his shift the next day. I said absolutely not. He then walked into the kitchen, filled a pan to the brim with water, came back into the living room where I sat on the couch, and dumped the water on my head.

Jordan walked into the living room one night and informed us all that AC/DC had just come to life through the poster on his wall and played a private concert for him in his bedroom. He said, "The notes from the songs they were playing turned into colors ... like gold and pink and this really light green ... and then the colors turned into smells like vanilla and strawberry and freshly cut grass ..." We all agreed that such a story could not simply be the result of too many vodka tonics. The next day Jordan confirmed our suspicions when he told us he had been tripping on shrooms.

Sweet roommates.

Because our place was the usual spot for the Sidewalks in Hell after-party, a lot of people used our living room as a crash landing pad after a long night. There were also people Hunter called the "street freaks"—random strangers who heard we rarely locked our doors and stumbled up to our place after a night at the bars. It was a great way to avoid paying taxi fare. For this reason I made sure to lock my bedroom door every night.

One morning a freak woke me up with a bloodcurdling scream. Careful to hurdle the empty beer bottles on the hallway floor, I sprinted to the bathroom, where the scream had originated.

I banged on the door until someone unlocked it to reveal a Chad furiously splashing water on his face. A redheaded Trixie had her arm wrapped lovingly around his waist and was trying to calm him down.

"What happened?" I asked.

"He had a little accident," the Trixie said. "Last night when he took out his contacts, he thought he put them in contact solution, but he accidentally put them in rubbing alcohol."

"I can't see! I'm blind!" the unfortunate Chad shouted.

"You'll be fine," the Trixie said. "Just keep splashing water on your eyes." She turned to me and said, "Apparently he doesn't remember anything about last night." The tone of her voice told me there was something she wished he remembered.

"Are you two friends with someone who lives here?" I asked.

"Um ... yeah." The Trixie's eyes quickly shifted to the left, but I couldn't remember from my criminal justice classes if a glance to the left meant the person was lying or telling the truth.

"Doesn't ... um, yeah ... Scott lives here ..." she said, in a way that sounded more like a question than a statement. But perhaps I had prematurely judged them. Maybe they were Scott's friends. Most freaks didn't get a name right; they usually first tried, "Yeah, I know Chad."

"So you're friends with Scott?" I asked as I handed the Chad a new washcloth from the linen closet.

"Yeah," the Trixie said. "We've both known Scott ... ever since he was a bartender at Wise Fool's." The Chad nodded in agreement between splashes. I was wise and would not be taken for a fool; Scott had never worked there. My bathroom was officially full of lies and the lying liars who told them.

The Trixie then turned back to the Chad and said, "I can't believe you were *that* drunk last night."

"Believe it," he said.

"I knew I should have cut you off," she said. "I swear, Jackson, you never know when to stop."

I didn't bother to ask if this guy was *the* Jackson, as in Haley's Jackson, because I already knew the answer.

Many nights after Kyle closed up The Bar at four in the morning, he and I walked together from The Bar to Mexicana Fiesta, where the owner, one of his regulars, hooked us up with chicken tacos and enchiladas. The best part was that he always gave us horchatas to take with us and drink on our walk home. Kyle was easily the person I most enjoyed talking to in all of Chicago, to the point that I was beginning to forget I no longer had Rachel. There was no *When Harry Met Sally* weirdness between Kyle and me. Kyle was still crazy about his first love from high school, a girl named Gretchen. He talked about her all the time and told me he would wait for her forever.

Kyle was a good friend to me. He even tried posting a cleaning schedule for the apartment the week I moved in. When Hunter saw it, he let out an evil cackle, tore it off the wall, and that was the end of that. But it was the thought that counted. Kyle used his bar hookups to get me free tickets to Bulls, Cubs, and Bears games. I surprised myself when I decided to invite Haley to go to a couple games with me. With the exception of her play-by-play critique of fashion faux pas she saw in the stadium, we actually had a nice time together, and I enjoyed her company.

I once mentioned to Kyle that when I lived at home, my mom made me eggs, bacon, and French toast every Sunday night for dinner. I would eat my "breakfast" at about nine o'clock while reading the Sunday newspaper. The next Sunday night, I came home to our apartment to find that Kyle had prepared me a feast of eggs, bacon, and French toast. He had even bought me a copy of the *Tribune*. "It was the best I could do," Kyle said. His "home away from home" gesture brought tears to my eyes.

I liked Bria, but I rarely saw her. Most nights she hibernated behind the closed door of her bedroom. In one of few conversations I had with her, I learned she had attended a small private college in Ohio and was now a third-grade teacher. Her boyfriend lived in Wrigleyville, and she was active in a nearby church. She invited me to go to church with her anytime.

I wanted to prove my theory. I believed there was little difference between the business of "the business" and the business of religion. I wanted to see firsthand if churches employed the same psychological techniques "the business" had used to control group behavior. The friendly people, positive mood, upbeat music, testimonies of changed lives, immediate call to action—these were all strategies I had only seen duplicated in houses of worship. But I hadn't been to church in a while, and I wanted to go again just to make sure I wasn't being too harsh.

Bria's church met in a Lakeview bar. A few smiling Trixies greeted us at the door and pointed to a corner where we could get coffee. Loud rock music blasted from overhead speakers above mingling twentysomethings in designer clothes. So far, my theory was proving true.

A girl sang a Sarah McLachlan cover song to kick things off. I was a big Sarah fan, and although I found it an odd song choice for church, I enjoyed it. However, I would have liked it better without the singer's excessive bravado and hyper-awareness of how the crowd perceived her. The guy who took the stage after her was no different. He offered a prayer in which he tried to fit four-syllable words into sentences where they didn't belong, in order to sound more intellectual. Unfortunately, he missed the mark terribly—as most people who try excessively tend to do.

The longer I sat there, the less Bria's church reminded me of "the business" and the more it reminded me of a bar. I got the impression that people were only there to see and be seen. They were all conscious of the way they looked and acted, as if it were an average night at the meat market. All that was missing was a couple of bouncers and a DJ spinning a Ludacris song.

After the academic's dissertation-disguised-as-a-prayer, two guys and three girls who comprised the "worship band" took the stage. They were there to lead everyone in "worship" songs, but unfortunately they had contracted the same look-at-me virus that afflicted the other church leaders and members. The "worship team" was nothing but a huge distraction.

The lyrics, when deconstructed, seemed to amount to very little. We sang about being in a "secret, quiet place" and how "in the stillness, God was there," ironically played on two electric guitars and a set of drums with speakers on high volume. Other worship songs were somewhat cryptic, yet the audience readily belted out each and every enigmatic word: "let the river flow," "fire fall down on me," "come be the air I breathe." It sounded like a science lesson on the elements. Other songs were dishonest, with lyrics like "God, You're all I want ..." Everyone in the room also clearly wanted a date for Friday night. Then came "I could sing of Your love forever ..." But, honestly, could they really?

After worship, the thirtysomething pastor stepped onto the stage and shouted, "How many of you can honestly say that Jesus is *the Man* tonight?" As everyone around me shouted enthusiastically, I wanted to scream, "Are you kidding me?"

The pastor continued, "I know how you guys get when you watch football games on Saturday. Big Ten schools don't mess around. You guys get all excited and loud during the game. So I think you should be able to get *at least* that excited and loud about Jesus on Sunday. Let me hear you make some noise!" The crowd again went nuts. I remembered hearing the same ludicrous football analogy in a Sunday school class ... in third grade. While it was slightly comforting that churches were still rehashing the same material, it was less comforting that not third-graders, but grown adults were responding so eagerly to something that really didn't make a whole lot of sense.

Another football/church analogy actually appealed to me. This one compared many churches to giant pep rallies. People go to have a loud, hyper-emotional time and get pumped up about the game. It is a way for non-players to have an exciting experience without committing to the daily lifestyle of an actual football player. The pep rally psychs everyone up for the game, but the players themselves are the only ones strong enough and prepared enough to actually *play*. They have trained for months or years. They have memorized the playbook, spent countless hours talking strategy with the coach, drilled their minds, and disciplined their bodies by practicing two, maybe three times per day—even when they don't feel like it—until their entire lives are consumed by football. Insert the obvious rest of the analogy.

To avoid the prolonged stares of a Chad in my row, I looked down to read the bulletin. On the front page was a picture of the same young pastor and a personal greeting. The headline read, "This Is Not Your Average Church." It explained that this church was nothing like the stuffy, traditional, and legalistic churches of previous generations. There was a picture of a tattooed, smiling girl with her lip and eyebrow pierced. She had her arm around a Trixie wearing a Juicy Couture shirt. The picture was clearly posed. Next to the picture were the words "We accept everyone just like they are. Period." I thought that the sentence might be better with a comma rather than a period: "We accept everyone just like they are, and *then* we teach them the Word of God so they can grow and change and become a much better person than the person they were." But what did I know?

The pastor's greeting also said in bold letters that "the old way of doing church absolutely does *not* work." It said, "This church is not like other intolerant churches you may have come across. We refuse to accept antiquated religious ideology" (a bit of an oxymoron).

I supposed some very legalistic churches had effectively forced churches like this one to go to extremes to prove they were indeed in touch with reality. Yet it seemed like this church was going to great lengths to fight the idea of "church" as the average person perceived it—without asking if that fight really deserved all their time and energy. I wondered if they had ever stopped to ask themselves if they might actually be fighting the *wrong* evil.

I was reminded of something else I had read in *The Myth of Certainty*. Daniel Taylor said,

> Many wounded Christians have a sarcastic bite to their use of the phrase "the church." ... Whether through their exposure to secular critics of religion, their greater intelligence or their broader experience, they have thankfully been liberated from the pathetic narrowness which still afflicts others. Adapting the superior attitude they elsewhere condemn, they, like the Pharisees in Christ's parable (Luke 18:11) thank God that they are not like other Christians: narrow, legalistic, and unsophisticated ... But what can the arrogant man or woman learn? Who can teach the smug and self-satisfied?

The church bulletin listed choices for Sunday school classes. Women had two options: "How to raise low self-esteem" and "Healing from broken relationships." I didn't think I would benefit much from either class. The two options for men were "Help with sexual integrity" and "Incorporating God into your corporate life." This reduction of an entire sex was a little troubling.

After the worship band finished, a Trixie took the microphone to announce some ongoing Sunday night support groups, including "Healing from an abortion," "Living with an eating disorder," and "Help after divorce." She said, "Remember that AA, Alanon, NA, and Celebrate Recovery groups also meet on a weekly basis." This didn't feel like a church; it felt like the self-help section of Barnes & Noble.

The young pastor then preached a four-point sermon that turned the word "hope" into a clever acrostic. He referenced a Scripture every now and then for good measure, but he swiftly bounced back to reality with examples specific to his target market: "Let's say you feel like you have no hope because you missed the fall sale at Marshall Field's ..."

The pastor used several movie clips during his message. I suppose he used them to reiterate that the church was in touch with contemporary culture, but they were just as distracting and pointless as the worship team had been. Plus, I could always catch the ten fifteen show at Landmark Century Theater after church.

Criticism is usually a waste of energy, especially when that energy could be used to seek out ways to right things. I didn't want to be judgmental. Nonetheless, I was collecting a cornucopia of criticism in my cranium. And I was starting to think in alliteration like the pastor's subpoints in his HOPE acrostic. The picture I had in my head of church might have included the psychological persuasion techniques I despised, but at least it included some solid teaching from the Bible.

I thought 2 Timothy 4:3 would be especially appropriate: "For the time will come when men will not put up with sound doctrine. Instead, to suit their own desires, they will gather around them a great number of teachers to say what their itching ears want to hear" (NIV).

Apparently, detailed Bible-teaching wasn't too popular. The older generation had purpose-driven megachurches with their never-ending building projects, and the younger generation had movie nights at the bar. Lengthy explanation of biblical passages had long since lost the battle to quick life applications for impatient listeners.

It was good that this church tried to meet the needs of hurting people. But I also wondered if any church whose members had actually grown in their faith (by reading and comprehending the Bible) would require as many ongoing classes and support groups as this church did. I didn't naïvely think that just teaching Scripture would stop all addiction and sexual temptation, but disciplined study of the Bible should provoke people to move past those types of basic unhealthy coping vices. The very fact that there was a support group for every possible poor choice in life almost felt like a permission slip to make those idiotic choices. It was authorization to stay stuck in the immaturity that plagued the rest of society.

The pastor gave me the distinct impression that he didn't think the Bible was enough—like he couldn't just preach from the Bible and still expect his audience to remain awake. The bulletin said that this church was "seeker-sensitive." But "seeker" didn't equal "stupid." I kind of thought that most seekers would be interested in learning what the Bible had to say, as opposed to hearing some mildly funny anecdotes from the pastor's personal life—anecdotes that he somehow managed to weave together and point back to "hope."

I wanted this church to know most people would be intelligent enough to rise to the occasion should the pastor try to explain the historical context of a chapter in Scripture. We didn't need another lesson about boundaries in relationships or how to handle our personal finances. We could go to the Borders bookstore on the corner for that. We needed to understand what the Bible teaches. Isn't that what the real purpose of the church is supposed to be?

After the service ended, I accompanied Bria and her small-group girls to a bar and grill. I wasn't surprised when they all ordered Cosmopolitans and started talking about boys and embarrassing drunken moments at John Barleycorn's. The tales of hooking up were plentiful and sordid. I wondered if anyone at the table had ever heard the verse 2 Timothy 2:22: "Flee the evil desires of youth, and pursue righteousness, faith, love and peace" (NIV).

The only deviation from hookups happened when one girl described a missions trip she took to India. She kept referring to the people she had met there as being "lost": "It was so sad to see how lost everyone was ... I have such a heart for the lost now that I've met so many people who don't know Christ." I thought about Jordan, Haley, and the rest of my coworkers. They would never classify themselves as "lost." They were perfectly content with the lives they had chosen. They weren't searching for anything.

The "lost" girl then went on to talk about her most recent Louis Vuitton purchase. Jumping from a story about orphans in Calcutta to a description of her new $300 wallet seemed more "lost" to me than anything she had described about India. And here I thought Hunter would have mocked me for going to church. If he had come to church with me, he would have fit right in. Aside from the occasional Christian buzzword, these people lived no differently than he did.

Hedonism reigned.

I guess if I wanted an old-school church experience, altar call and all, I'd have to return to one of Kenya's business meetings.

"You should start coming to our Tuesday night small group," one of Bria's friends said to me. "The study we're going through right now has given me a new outlook. It's really shown me what being a Christian is all about."

I wanted to tell the girl that I didn't need her small group to change my outlook. Four illegal immigrants, an Islamic ex-con, a Yugoslavian agnostic, a bartender, and a Buddhist semi-pro wrestler had already shown me what being a Christian was all about.

"Thanks for the invite," I said. "But I have to work on Tuesday nights."

ELEVEN

HOW SHALL **WE** THEN **LIVE?**

"The greatest bores are men who go about trying to change the world without first trying to change themselves."
—Thoreau

My friend Sebastian walked into a Git-n-Go one day and bought some Zebra Cakes and one of those ginseng tea drinks with a label that says, "Improves Memory Power." As he left the store, the clerk followed him out, shouting, "Sir, you forgot your drink!"

Later, Sebastian managed to successfully memorize the first two hundred digits of pi. This feat won him looks of intrigue and interest from many friends, which then morphed into looks of boredom as Sebastian began dutifully reciting the two hundred numbers.

Knowing Sebastian's history of constantly trying to better his mind, I thought he'd be a good person to ask a question I couldn't answer. I wanted to know whether it was okay to go along with the stupidity of our mainstream culture to avoid being labeled as judgmental, or if it was wiser to withdraw from culture to the greatest extent possible, to prove that you don't condone the direction our society is heading. Sebastian told me that in every choice, there is always a third option. He said Jesus Christ Himself exemplified that third option when He came to earth. He sought neither to conform to society nor to withdraw from it—He sought instead to *change* it.

I saw this as a central problem with organized religion. They erred on one side or the other, forgetting the third option. A man named Claudio Letelier once wrote a letter to the *Los Angeles Times* saying, "I am a visitor from Chile, and this is my first trip to your country. I find many things to admire ... However, I am more than puzzled by the incredibly low intellectual and cultural standards of the American people which, in many ways, translate themselves into a kind of television programming that, frankly, is not keeping with the tastes and requirements of an educated nation."

No kidding?

You mean to tell me that my loyalty to shows like *Seinfeld* didn't cause you to associate me with a philosophic subset superior to those who don't understand nihilism in action?

The Chilean's letter is nothing new. Other nations have expressed, many times over the past decades, how shocked and appalled they are with America—not just with our mass media, but also with our lack of connection to each other and to our communities (probably thanks to mass media). They question our mixed-up morals and priorities, selfish lifestyles, and excessive consumerism. Yet we often feel powerless to change things. Furthermore, we believe that even just talking about changing things somehow makes us appear non-progressive, narrow-minded, and foolish.

So we say nothing.

The best part about living in a city is that the beauty of humanity is everywhere.

Sitting at my usual table on the patio of Dunkin' Donuts, I was surrounded by emotion.

Infatuation was to my right. A couple at the table next to me were kissing passionately and looking at each other in a way that proved the phrase "starry-eyed" wasn't just a cliché.

Anger was across the street. Another couple stood on the corner, arms loaded with bags after a long day of shopping. They were arguing in low tones, getting progressively louder by the minute.

Boredom was at the bus stop. Waiting tables wasn't the only kind of waiting that happened in the city. People were waiting all the time, for the bus, the L, an empty taxi ... I saw bored people fidgeting at the bus stop across the street, scrolling through their cell phonebooks to find someone they could call to pass the time.

A hunger for knowledge lined the sidewalks. People sat at outdoor tables reading newspapers, magazines, and books.

Joy passed by. A Trixie walking by me squealed into the mouthpiece of her cell phone: "You are never going to believe who called me last night!"

Seduction was in bloom at the sushi place across the street. It still irritated me that girls at the height of immaturity adored bad boys, but I accepted it as part of the life cycle. Although they hadn't spotted me yet, from where I sat, I could see Hunter and Jordan dining on the patio of my favorite sushi restaurant with two giggling Trixies they had met just ten minutes prior.

Love was in front of me. I watched a little boy, probably four years old, running down the sidewalk in tears as he called out over and over for his mother. He was clearly lost. He finally stood motionless, sobbing, not knowing where to run next as people passed him by. Then two tall Eastern European-looking men who barely spoke English stooped down next to him. They patted his head lovingly and said, "We'll stay with you until you find your mom. You don't need to cry. You're safe now." As the boy looked up into the faces of these kind strangers, his tears instantly stopped. At that moment, my tears began. It was one of the more beautiful scenes I had ever watched unfold—a tiny child between two large strangers from another country, each holding one of his hands. They walked with him down the street until he was reunited with his thankful mother.

I was beginning to accept that often strangers are the angels that make us feel safe when we are lost and alone.

But there is a downside to this up-close-and-personal view of humanity that accompanies city life. In a non-urban area, a person can leave the house and get directly into his car, still sheltered from the world while going from place to place. But in a city, a person relinquishes that safety and control. A quick errand to the store can be a mentally and emotionally draining task because there is no bubble to protect him from the outside world. No one is exempt from the beggar holding up his hand or the scam artist charging $55 for a shoeshine. Even if a person is just taking a thirty-second walk to the corner store for toilet paper and milk, he probably won't go unscathed. And even if the person is fortunate enough to avoid outright confrontation with the marginalized, there are still dozens of lonely looks and angry attitudes of passersby to contend with.

After a while, the only way to get through the day was to dismiss those sights. Either that, or spend all day listening to strangers' stories: "My daughter has a bad heart. I need money to pay for her heart transplant," or "My husband just died, and I can't pay the bills."

A woman in tears once approached Rachel and me on the street. She said she was running from her abusive husband who might find her and kill her at any moment unless we could spare $3 so she could take the bus to a suburb where her sister lived. She showed us bruises on her arm—the result, she claimed, of her husband "grabbing" her. Never mind that the bruises looked more like the work of a needle maneuvered by the hands of a heroin addict.

The woman insisted it was up to Rachel and me to save her from certain death.

As Rachel reached into her purse, fishing for some change, the woman said, "Oh, and one more thing—if you could also pay for my six kids to ride the bus with me to my sister's house, that would be great." She said her kids were waiting for her just a few blocks away.

Knowing full well there were no children waiting, I said, "Why don't we walk with you to get your kids, and then we can make sure you all get on the bus together." The woman abruptly stopped crying, shot me a dirty look, and said, "I don't think so," and mumbled an angry string of obscenities as she hurried away.

The challenge presented to the city dweller was whether to be compassionate and stupid or uninvolved and street-smart. Inaction was the favored choice because it could be easily justified with remarks like "I saw this news special about some homeless guy in Chicago who made $80,000 a year begging on the sidewalks."

Visitors to the White House in Washington, D.C., learn that a homeless woman named Conchita has lived a stone's throw from the front lawn for more than two decades. Her home is a little tent encircled by cardboard signs protesting nuclear war. The only reason most people notice Conchita at all is that they accidentally stumble across her humble abode while on their way to the White House. This is how it is in Chicago as well. En route to somewhere pleasant, people are continually stumbling across the unpleasant.

From my table at Dunkin' Donuts, I saw pain in the doorway of a bank. A homeless man with thick dirt caked in his hair held up a broken plastic cup to busy Lincoln Park residents as they exited the bank. Most people who passed him were talking on their cell phones and didn't notice his raised arm. A guy walking with his arm around his girlfriend dropped his arm to reach for his wallet. His girlfriend smacked his hand away, and they continued on. A Trixie passing by turned to her friend and said, "That is so disgusting. Don't they know we don't want to see that stuff?" But not even Trixies could escape the lessons of the city.

Desperation was so close I could smell it. Next to me a homeless man in his boxers was rummaging through the Dunkin' Donuts garbage can. He pulled out a Styrofoam cup still half full of coffee. I could smell that it was hazelnut. He removed the lid and drank it down in one long gulp.

Whenever I became extremely frustrated with not only the economic disparity all around me, but also the lack of a "right way" to handle it, I thought about Conchita's little tent pitched right next to the White House and was reminded of a saying I had heard once: "After the game, the king and the pawn go back into the same box."

When I first moved to Chicago, I thought a lot about John Mayer's lyrics, "I just found out there's no such thing as the real world ... just a lie you've got to rise above." Now, with all that had happened, I moved on to think about other song lyrics of his, like "'Everything happens for a reason' is no reason not to ask myself if I am living it right."

I hadn't returned to church with Bria. But every now and then I asked how her small group was going. "Do you girls take turns leading the discussion each week?" I asked.

"Actually, Tarrah's been leading it for the last few months," Bria said. "But she's been out of town a lot lately, so Keri's been filling in."

"Did I meet Tarrah?" I asked.

"No, she wasn't there the night you came. You'll have to meet her sometime though. I actually just went over to her apartment last night to see pictures from her most recent trip to Washington, D.C."

"Most recent? Does she go there a lot?"

"She goes there every so often to report on this project thing she's been working on for the U.S. government. This last time she went, she got to meet the president."

"You actually *saw* pictures of her with the president?" I asked.

Bria gave me a weird look, not understanding why I was so dubious of a stranger. "Yeah, I saw them," she said. "They were shaking hands in the Oval Office. Why? Do you know her or something?"

"Did she tell you her project was top-secret?" I asked.

"Yeah ... it's got something to do with national security," Bria said. "But what's not a secret anymore is how much money Tarrah's going to make on the project as soon as she releases it to the government. I just read an article about it in the newspaper the other day."

"How much is she going to make?" I asked.

"About $25 million," Bria said.

"Will you do me a favor?" I asked. Bria hesitantly nodded yes.

"Will you go into the kitchen right now and tell Hunter everything you just told me?"

I couldn't wait to see Hunter's face when he learned that Tarrah would soon be the richest regular at Paronelli's. Tarrah had hardly been working on Operation Goof Troop.

I love gas stations—truck stops especially—for frozen Cokes, bathroom breaks, thirty kinds of beef jerky.

Once, Rachel and I pulled away from a gas station with the pump still in our gas tank. We dragged it a few blocks before "that weird bumping noise" grew loud enough to warrant our attention.

My favorite gas station, though, was somewhere in the heart of Kentucky. Rachel and I, along with three other friends, were en route to spring break in South Padre when we decided to take a pit stop in the middle of nowhere. It was three o'clock in the morning, and we had already been driving fourteen hours. We thought a quick dose of fluorescent lights and actual signs of life would wake us up. We did not expect, however, to step from the dark of night and the calming smooth jazz music on our car radio into the all-out *carnival* that was taking place at this particular gas station.

People were everywhere. There were individuals watching TV, taking showers, sitting in a café eating stuffed-crust pizza, playing pinball and air hockey, shopping for a bedspread (why there were bedspreads available for purchase, we'll never know), arguing over which DVDs to buy, comparing and contrasting the various kinds of Native American dreamcatchers for sale, reading the paper, and making their own ice cream sundaes. Truckers were sharing information; children were playing hide and seek in the aisles; and through it all, John Mellencamp sang loudly over the speakers, "Ain't that America ... somethin' to see ..."

One trucker was talking to a clerk about the unusually high number of skunks he had smelled since crossing the Kentucky border. "It's crazy; their scent is so strong out here," he said. "I can smell them coming from miles away." I felt like I needed to get involved in the conversation, especially after I realized the trucker was ascertaining that the skunks in Kentucky had somehow acquired a more pungent odor than the skunks in the other forty-nine states. I told the man I actually liked the smell of skunk because it reminded me of the open road, to which he replied, "Well, I'll be thrown on the gravel and run over by a tractor trailer!" He said it so loud that Rachel heard his response from where she sat in her restroom stall. I could hear echoes of her laughter bouncing off the bathroom walls. Just ten minutes prior, I had been tired of driving, nearly lulled to sleep by the car's steady humming rhythm over the pavement. But now I was invigorated and hyper-alert as I discussed skunk conspiracy theories with a trucker and a gas station attendant.

But gas stations in Chicago were nothing like my favorite gas station in Kentucky. They were cold and had very little personality. They were all business, with their stern "Pay before you pump" signs. I hated sliding my money into the little metal receptacle under the bulletproof glass window. I hated feeling like I had just made some type of illegal exchange every time I drove away from the gas station. I wanted to find one, just *one*, gas station in Chicago that would let me pay *after* I pumped and wouldn't make me feel like such a criminal during the exchange process. I wanted a gas station that had a little faith in the residents of the city, one that would dare to believe Chicagoans might be a trustworthy bunch of people after all. But maybe that was asking too much. I vacillated between loving and hating the city. But I supposed that I, like everyone else around me, was just looking for some prolonged peace.

I was walking along Michigan Avenue one day when I saw a man handing out tracts to busy shoppers. He wore a nametag that said "Bill," and he was part of a group of twenty people stationed on different street corners downtown. They were instructed to hand out tracts and ask passersby, "Do you know what would happen if you died tonight?"

A punk kid with a Mohawk looked at Bill and said, "Dude, I tried reading the Bible a few years ago, but it was too confusing. Then I tried attending a church here in town, but it freaked me out. Everybody was speaking some crazy language, and people were falling on the ground ... the pastor called it being 'slain in the Spirit.' Now that's some seriously freaky [stuff]. So then I tried praying to God one night. I asked Him to lead me to the truth, but nothing happened."

Bill cocked his head to the side and looked at the boy with pity. "You're wrong," he said. "Something did happen. God brought you here to meet me."

The punk kid laughed nervously.

"I'll tell you what," Bill said. "Let's pray together right now. Maybe you just didn't have enough faith the first time you prayed. But if we take thirty seconds to pray right now, you can be sure you're going to heaven when you die."

"Seriously?" Mr. Mohawk said. "You're telling me a thirty-second prayer is all it takes?" He was being sarcastic, but Bill hadn't detected it.

"I promise, that's all it takes," Bill said. "I prayed that same prayer years ago, and now I'm absolutely sure I'm going to heaven when I die. Will you pray with me?"

"Nope. Thanks anyway, dude."

In *The Myth of Certainty*, Daniel Taylor said,

> Much of the church has sold out to the myth of certainty. We are told by the rationalistic Christian, "We don't have to float around like the poor secularist, because we have

absolutes. The secularist lost his absolutes when he got rid of God. Because God is our absolute, our truth claims are certain, not contingent; objective, not subjective; eternal, not temporal." The careful Christian apologist realizes that belief in absolutes is just that, a belief (and justifiable as such I hasten to add), but the typical Christian in the pew is left with the distinct impression that absolutes give us certainty about the things of faith. In order to promote this feeling of certainty, conservative Christendom erects an elaborate system of apologetics, group psychology and often legalism. Even the reflective person often succumbs to the false either-or of institutional belief: "Either you have the certainty about God and His will that we do, or you are possibly not even a believer at all." As a result, many either try to "believe harder," seeking the tranquil unquestioning that seems the ideal, or, out of a sense of confused integrity, sever themselves from the church whose standard they cannot meet.

Certainty may not be possible. However, the fact that we can't be certain about anything in life should not stop us from believing. We are still capable of acquiring enough information to compel us to believe that something is the truth. Our problem is often simply a lack of good information.

Years after leaving Chicago, I finally found a place where I was able to gather good information about the Christian faith. Unlike Bria's church or the street corner where Bill encouraged blind belief, I found a place where I learned what the Bible has to say, verse by verse, so that I could make a rational decision whether or not to believe.

I learned the biblical history of Israel and the details of the Jewish faith and traditions—knowledge that was key in helping me fully understand Christianity (not to mention current events in the Middle East). I learned Old Testament verses in their original Hebrew and New Testament verses in their original Greek to get as close to the true meaning as possible. I learned the personalities and backgrounds of the Bible's forty-plus authors, who were kings, doctors, shepherds, teachers, fishermen, farmers, musicians, philosophers, poets, and priests. This helped me to better understand their unique writing styles. I learned specifics about the Bible's covenants, as well as the messages of the prophets. I learned about the various empires throughout history—the Egyptians, Assyrians, Babylonians, Persians, Greeks—and how each played a role in the 1,500 years that the Bible covers. I learned the customs, traditions, and ideologies of the Roman Empire, which was the ruling empire throughout the life of Jesus. Just as a thorough understanding of our culture today would shed light on the way we live our lives, knowing what the culture was like in Jesus' day can give us important new insights.

And all of this I learned in a shop teacher's living room. A man named Galyn Wiemers, a full-time high-school teacher with a wife and six sons, had recognized that many people have no real idea what the Bible has to say—including people who've sat through hundreds of church sermons. So he began teaching in his living room several nights a week for anyone interested in learning about the Bible. As we worked through each book, the story began to take shape, and, remarkably enough, that story also began to make sense.

A girl with a long flowing skirt and henna designs stretching from her fingertips to her elbows walked past Bill, who was still eagerly handing out tracts.

"Can I ask you a question?" Bill asked.

"Can I first ask *you* a question?" the girl replied.

"I guess," Bill said, looking confused.

"What do you think you'll be in your next life?" she asked.

Bill grimaced.

"I'll make you a deal," she said. "I'll read your Bible if you'll read the Bhagavad Gita. And I'll worship your God if you'll worship Brahma."

With disgust, Bill said no, and the girl continued walking.

Bill's next victim was an older man who possessed that refined, well-educated, "professor" quality.

"Do you know what would happen if you died tonight?" Bill asked him.

"I know my wife would be a lot happier," the man said, smiling.

"You know, if you believe in Jesus, you'll go to heaven when you die," Bill said, getting right down to business.

"Great then," the man said. "Jesus is a historically well-documented figure, and I've always believed He existed. I even believe He died on a cross. So I guess I'll see you in heaven."

"It ..." Bill stammered. "It's not just belief in Jesus ... it's ..."

Bill could not clarify what "believing in Jesus" really meant. I wanted to help the poor guy by explaining that believing Jesus existed is common sense, but believing Jesus is *the Christ* is what this faith is all about. In the Old Testament, God told the Jews that through their lineage would come a Messiah who would reign forever. To *believe* in Jesus means to believe He was and is the promised Messiah.

"Here's how I see it," the man said to Bill. "If I end up in heaven, that's great. If I end up in hell, that's great too. I'm sure I'll have plenty of friends down there, and at least I won't have to spend eternity with my wife."

The man whistled a tune as he walked away.

Bill wearily stopped yet another stranger, a young college student. "Can I ask you a quick question?"

"Uh ... not today," the student said. "I'm pressed for time."

"You don't have time for God?" Bill asked.

"Sorry, shopping is top priority right now."

As I gazed down the street at people walking in and out of stores, I realized the student had been the voice of the masses.

TWELVE

THE DOCTOR'S WISDOM

"God will be present, whether asked or not."
—Latin Proverb

I met a customer at Paronelli's who worked for the biggest juvenile justice agency in the state of Illinois. She told me she might have a job for me as a crisis counselor for youth in the Chicago housing projects.

A *real* job at last.

On Monday, I interviewed. On Wednesday I received a job offer. On Friday, in a completely unrelated incident, I got fired from Paronelli's.

Brad fired me.

It was a big miscommunication, a mix-up between Jordan and me about who was covering a shift for Haley. I'm still not exactly sure what happened. But I *am* sure I got fired. And, unlike Hunter, I didn't get rehired.

Despite my bitterness, I had to admit that once again, the timing could not have been more perfect. Had I been fired just a week earlier, I would not have met the Paronelli's customer who got me the job—the real job I'd been hoping for since the first day I moved to Chicago. The job I'd actually spent four years in college to become qualified for.

Hunter, Jordan, Kyle, and Scott started bowing to me every time they saw me. They said I was their hero. "You're the first person to ever inspire Brad to *act* like a real manager," Hunter said. They were planning a little party at The Bar in honor of my esteemed accomplishment.

I was about to go from waiting tables at Paronelli's to counseling kids from the projects. No longer would I experience Trixies talking about the latest neighborhood gossip, but rather Gangsta's Disciples talking about the latest drive-by shooting.

My daily conversations wouldn't revolve around Haley's shoes, Mark's cat, or religious and philosophic ideology. Instead, my days would soon be filled with exchanges such as:

> Me: Why didn't you go to school today, Steve?
> Steve: 'Cause the hos was out.

> Me: Glen, why'd you pull a knife on Will?
> Glen: 'Cause he was frontin' my nation, yo!

> Me: Alana, where were you last night?
> Alana: I was out trickin.' Where else would I be?

My job's jargon—which had previously involved expressions like "two-top," "comp," or "joiner"—was about to change drastically as well. I was getting ready to re-enter the world of social services, a world where absolutely everything is abbreviated and the two most overused words are "tool" and "piece"—as in, "I found the screening test to be a great tool for the prevention piece."

Additionally, I would need to learn the language of my new clientele. I would be taught that a "dime" wasn't a coin—it was a reference to an attractive female. And if a guy was "about to rotate," his activities had nothing to do with car tires. He would, however, soon be leaving the building.

As a crisis counselor, I would intervene whenever a kid ended up at a Chicago police station or psychiatric hospital due to any type of crisis. "Crisis" was obviously a broad, catch-all term. I would mediate if a parent abused a child ... or if a child tried to kill a parent. There would be a spectrum of crises.

In my first month on the job, the following kids were assigned as part of my caseload:

1. Alana, a pregnant sixteen-year-old who had been picked up by the police for the ninth time on a prostitution charge. Alana was eventually sent to a psychiatric hospital where, after smoking crack one day, she set fire to the building, injuring three people.

2. Steve, a sixteen-year-old who was well-respected in the Gangsta's Disciples. After being put on probation for drug charges and possession of weapons, Steve did some time after stealing a car. He stole it so he could drive to Mexico to escape his psychotic mother, Janine, who held a gun to his head every night until he finished his chores.

3. Darcy, a manic-depressive fourteen-year-old who had been kicked out of her house because she refused to abort her baby. Darcy was one of nine children, all of whom shared the same thirty-three-year-old biological mother. Darcy had tried to commit suicide four times since her twelfth birthday.

4. Misha, an eleven-year-old girl who was molested by her stepfather and her uncle on a regular basis. When Misha told her mother about the molestation, her mother dropped her off at a police station and told me and the juvenile officer, "I never want to see her again. Don't call me to tell me where she ends up. Just

make sure I never see this child or hear about her whereabouts again. You understand?"

5. Jerome and Glen, two fifteen-year-olds who were arrested before they could carry out the murder they were required to commit for the Latin Kings gang.

6. Kent, an eleven-year-old who had been molested by his father and who had, in turn, molested a seven-year-old girl. He had a major problem with cutting and had carved all sorts of occult symbols into his arms and legs.

7. Caroline, a fifteen-year-old whose mother, Rena, insisted Osama Bin Laden had their home under twenty-four-hour surveillance. For this reason she hadn't let Caroline leave the house in eight months. Rena had burned most of Caroline's clothing in their fireplace, insisting, "we must not leave any evidence for Al Qaeda to find."

8. Nick, a schizophrenic seventeen-year-old who, in a fit of anger, threw his mom against a wall so hard that it caused countless vertebrae to rupture in her back. He pulled a knife on his father and brother when they attempted to intervene.

9. Travis, a ten-year-old who was taken into custody for possession of cocaine and attempted to assault an officer while en route to the police department. Travis was a chronic runaway, having reportedly left home sixty-two times in one year.

Needless to say, my faith, or lack thereof, was going to face additional challenges in my new job. But if I had managed to uncover some reason to believe amidst the chaos of the city, I figured it was also possible to get a glimpse of God in the ghetto.

My eighteen months of working at Paronelli's had met with sudden death. There were certain things I would never again be able to experience. Like watching Mario salsa dance on the bar after we locked up for the night, or exchanging an eye roll with Haley as we listened to Brad recount his floating experience to yet another customer. Like listening to Abuelo whistle "You Light Up My Life" while he stocked the salad bar, or watching Hunter and Jordan cackle in unison after checking to see if they were still clocked in.

I would still see the guys at home, and I would catch up with everyone else at The Bar—but it would never be the same. I wouldn't spend as much time with Mark, but I would still try to live in the moment. I wouldn't be around Haley nearly as much, but I would keep in mind that some Trixies might not be so bad if I take the time to get to know them. I would rarely see Brad or Nola, but I would try to put myself in other people's shoes each time I didn't understand their worldviews. I would miss being around the cooks and Abu, but I would keep looking for teachers in unexpected places.

Hunter had once said that I was different from him because I was still naïve enough to think there was "something else out there better than this." Now I understood ... there was nothing more out there. A microcosm of the world was in a long, narrow Italian restaurant somewhere in Chicago. There were thousands of other places just like it.

When I told my college friend Drew that I had taken a job waiting tables, he said, "Life is all about waiting. We're all just sitting in one big waiting room ... not sure when we're going to be called in to see the doctor." Cheesy, but eerily true.

The terms "waiter" and "waitress" are virtually obsolete in the food industry, having been replaced with the unisex title of "server." Maybe there's a hidden lesson to be learned in the changing language—maybe those of us who have to wait should learn to serve ...

When I was ten years old, I was in love with Ryan. In fourth grade, he wore a white-washed denim jacket to school over his favorite tri-colored rugby shirt. He chased me around the playground at recess with the intention of kissing me. He and I often got kicked out of class together for flirting and passing notes. We had snowball fights, spit wad fights, and water balloon fights in an effort to express our true feelings for each other.

Over the years, friends had shared with me the latest rumors concerning Ryan's status and whereabouts.

"I heard Ryan grew a long, nasty beard." True.

"I heard Ryan contracted a life-threatening disease when he was in Venezuela." False.

"I heard Ryan can bench press 430 pounds, and it's because he's on steroids." First part true, second part false.

"I heard Ryan moved to Jerusalem to study theology." True.

The flying rumors didn't define my opinion of Ryan, mostly because I generally already had some firsthand knowledge. Ryan and I never completely lost touch over the years. We were on what we coined "the cycle." Ryan would call to tell me he wanted to be with me, and I would say no. Six months later I would tell him that I had made a mistake by turning him down, by which time it would be too late—he would no longer be interested. Fast-forward another six months, and on cue, he'd call me again to tell me he wanted to start a relationship. The cycle would start again.

As part of the six-month rotation, Ryan called me one year from a cruise ship en route to the Netherlands to profess his undying love. After about twenty minutes of conversation, he was in the middle of saying, "Look, I've obviously always known I would end up with you ..." when he stopped abruptly and said, "Oh, I just noticed a sign on the wall that says calls from this phone cost $10 per minute." I insisted we end the call. He said he didn't care about the money. I hung up on him. He called back. I told him I was dating someone else. He told me, "You know it will never work because you'll end up with me." I was furious and hung up again.

The next year I wrote Ryan a long letter telling him he was right and we probably were meant to be. This outpouring was the direct result of my friend Kris insisting I watch the movie *The Family Man*, in which Nicolas Cage's character gets a glimpse of what his life would have been like if he had married his one true love. As you might guess, his life without her is lonely and meaningless; with her, he is fulfilled and actually happy. Unfortunately, I was much too vulnerable to sappy movies—especially that pivotal final scene in romantic comedies that involves someone running through an airport to stop someone else from getting on a plane. I was determined to learn from Nicolas Cage's character's mistake. *I* would make the *right* choice. I would choose love before it was too late. I went home and wrote a long letter to Ryan, which proved inconsequential because I hadn't bothered to check whether or not he was dating someone else. My mistake.

Six months later, while cleaning out his college dorm room, Ryan found and reread my post-*Family Man* epiphany letter. By this time he was single again, and he called me immediately. Choosing to forego the customary greeting of "hello" for "I can't stop thinking about you," he asked me to attend a Tori Amos concert with him as our first official "date." (The Tori pick was a direct result of Ryan's I-want-my-music-tastes-to-match-my-melancholy stage of life, but I agreed to go anyway.) After this we talked regularly for the next few months—a connection that tapered off during his busy college football season.

Approximately six months later, Ryan and I took an impromptu road trip to see some friends. On the ride, we resolved to stop the never-ending cycle of romance between us, once and for all. It had continued for too long, and neither of us had been able to move on because of it. We both honored our agreement, and by the time I moved to Chicago, it had been a year since either of us had tried to make contact. The cycle was officially broken. And I was forced to chalk up more than a decade of madness to the adage "You never really get over your first love."

I stood in front of Dunkin' Donuts debating whether or not to go in. I only had a couple of free afternoons left before beginning my full-time job. I walked inside. Life was too short to deny myself even one Mocha Blast. I didn't have Rachel to talk to, but plenty of other familiar faces surrounded me—including Black Jesus, who was prophesying imminent doom to an uninterested taxi driver.

My cell phone started vibrating in my purse.

"Hello," I said, even though it was an unknown number.

"Hi." One word with only two letters had been spoken, but the voice was unmistakable.

"Whoa ... Ryan, what's up?"

"I called your parents to get your new number." Silence.

"Oh yeah?" It had been so long since we had last talked that I wasn't sure what to say.

"I'm coming to Chicago this weekend. I want to see you. I need to see you." Ryan wasn't partial to conjunctions. He spoke in short sentences. He was direct. He got to the point. I used to hate it. Today I liked it.

"Can I see you?" he asked.

All I could think was ... here we go again.

When I was ten, I believed I would marry Ryan. When I was ten, I also believed in God. I prayed every night, asking God to let Ryan and me end up together. Apparently, a child knows more truth than

I thought, and there must be a little more to prayer than I thought. Sixteen years later, Ryan and I were married.

Maxwell, the restaurant sage, had predicted that I was going to find my one true love.

I should have known that since I only ever had one true love to begin with, finding him would just mean finding him again.

When my friend Lora from Nixa, Missouri, asked how I felt about Ryan being back in my life, I had to say, "Sometimes you just know."

My two-minute walk to work was a thing of the past. I would now be driving to work. Although my office was a mere ten miles from my apartment, it would take at least an hour to get to work each morning, thanks to Chicago rush-hour traffic. I pulled away from the curb my first day, yawning and groggy.

As I turned the corner into the standstill line of cars waiting to pull onto Lake Shore Drive, the cab behind me honked loud and long, as though it were my fault we weren't going anywhere. I looked in my rearview mirror and shook my head at him.

And that's when I saw it.

I instantly picked up the phone and dialed Rachel's number. Surprisingly, she answered.

"Whoa," I said. "What are you doing up this early? I figured it would ring through to your voice mail."

"I'm getting an early start on apartment hunting today," she said. "I cannot *stand* one more week of living with my family. Seriously, Chloe's the only one I can handle right now." Chloe was her cat.

"That sucks," I said.

"The question is more like, what are *you* doing up so early?" Rachel asked. It was a first. We were both awake and coherent at such an early hour.

"Today's my first day of work," I said.

"Oh, that's right. I totally forgot," she said.

"But the reason I'm calling this early is because you will never guess what I saw just now while driving down the street."

"What'd you see?"

"Guess."

"Um ... you saw a bunch of Trixies coming out of Starbucks?"

"Yes, but that's not it. Guess again."

"Um, oh, I know ... you saw Brad floating down Lincoln Avenue at a forty-five-degree angle?"

"Excellent guess," I said. "Try again."

"You saw Dr. Porter shouting at passing traffic?"

"Now you're getting much warmer."

"If it has to do with Dr. Porter, don't make me guess anymore ... tell me *right* now." Rachel was excited.

"I think I just saw the Possibility Place," I said.

"What? There's no way," Rachel said.

"No, there is a way," I said. "When I looked in my rearview mirror a few seconds ago, I swear I saw a sign a few blocks back that said 'Possibility Place.'"

"Where was it?"

"On the same street we found Dr. Porter's nasty, empty store, which is all the more reason I think it might be legit."

"But that's one of the busiest streets in Lincoln Park," Rachel said. "If the Possibility Place were actually there, we would have seen it by now. I mean, we worked on that street. We would have walked right past the thing every day."

"I'm telling you, I really think I saw it," I said. "Maybe the store wasn't there a few months ago when we were both working nearby ... but I really think it's there now. Anyway, I'm turning the corner to go around the block and check it out."

"Good," Rachel said. "I'll wait."

"So what else is new there?" I asked.

"Nothing," Rachel said. "My family's annoying ... I need an apartment ... Landon keeps calling me. He and his brother Lee are coming to Minneapolis in a few weeks, and they want to see me."

"Don't do it."

"He told me that when he 'joins forces' with his brother, they're 'unstoppable' ... whatever that means ..."

"That guy is so weird," I said.

"It's the medieval haircut," Rachel said.

"No," I said. "Don't even *try* to act like you were on the medieval bandwagon with me. You were way too busy trying to figure out what 'mid-evil' meant."

"Shut up," Rachel said. "So what else is new with you?"

"Since we last talked yesterday, absolutely nothing," I said. "Oh, except Hunter met this random girl at the sushi place across from Dunkin' ... oh oops ..."

"What?"

"I'm in front of the sign I saw."

"And ..." Rachel waited with drumroll anxiety.

"My bad," I said. "I was wrong. The sign definitely does *not* say Possibility Place."

"I knew it!" Rachel said. "I knew there was no way that place existed. So what does the sign say?"

"Uh ..."

"Yes, spit it out."

"Paronelli's Pasta."

"What?" Rachel was laughing hysterically. "Don't you know what the Paronelli's sign looks like by now? You worked there for almost two years!"

"Well, I know what it *used* to look like," I said. "But sometime in the last three weeks they put up this ugly new sign I'm looking at right now."

"They tore down the old red one?" Rachel asked.

"Yeah," I said. "And they put up some weird white one with

black cursive letters you can barely read ... except that there are two big, distinct Ps at the beginning of each word ... which is why I thought it said 'Possibility Place.'"

Rachel was laughing. "Well, it's a good thing you didn't wake me up for this little debacle."

"Sorry," I said. "I'll call you on my way home from work."

"Thanks for giving me a laugh to start off the day," Rachel said. "I'll talk to you tonight."

I chalked up my mistake to drowsiness as I drove on past Paronelli's.

But as I continued down the street, I realized that the goal of my call to Rachel had still been met, although not in the way I had planned. I had called Rachel because I had wanted to let her know that maybe Dr. Porter wasn't so crazy after all.

And I think that's kind of what I told her.

Afterword

I recently stopped by Paronelli's after more than six years since working there. Other than a few new additions to the menu, not much has changed. Several of the same daily regulars were eating dinner. Mario, at his usual post cooking up some penne with marinara sauce, filled me in on the whereabouts of the old Paronelli's crew.

Mario, Juan (Abuelo), and Juan (Uno) are still diligently working at the restaurant. Mario said they were thankful last year when their hours were cut from ninety-six per week to only ninety.

Juan (Primo) moved back to Mexico to be with his family.

Abu still works at Paronelli's delivering food. His prearranged marriage is going well, and they adopted two children.

Mark still picks up an occasional shift at Paronelli's. He has a serious live-in girlfriend now who takes up a lot of his time. The Grim Reaper is obviously not yet a household name, but stay tuned.

Brad quit Paronelli's and moved back east to be near his family. Rumors suggest he may actually have been fired by Mr. Paronelli after a big disagreement, but no one knows for sure.

Haley got a job working at Saks Fifth Avenue. She stops by Paronelli's for a beer every now and then. Jackson moved to Denver, and they no longer talk.

Nola is the president of a GLBT community-outreach program. She broke up with Jade, but they are "sharing custody" of their dog Maylee (a pet they had purchased in lieu of having a baby).

Kyle is still working full time at The Bar Next Door. He is still waiting for Gretchen.

Scott now works for his father's company in a Chicago suburb. No one sees much of him.

Hunter and Jordan are both *still* waiting tables a couple of nights a week at Paronelli's. They have toured with Sidewalks in Hell and are still hoping to sign with a big label. Hunter also performs at Second City and now has an agent.

The old apartment where we lived is now inhabited by eight Trixies.

And, for all I know, Hunter and Jordan are probably still clocked in twenty-four/seven.

Oh, and Rachel got married. She has a job supervising caseworkers at a Minnesota social service agency. She's finally happy.